MW01714068

The Secret of Mixing Colors from *Angel Liana*

Written and Illustrated
by:

Dr. Rosemary Hartounian Cohen

Lico Publishing
1541 South Robertson Boulevard
Los Angeles, CA 90035

The Secret of Mixing Colors from Angel Liana

Rosemary Hartounian Cohen, Ph.D.
Author & Illustrator

Copyright© 2016 by Lico Publishing
Text copyright © 2016 by Rosemary Hartounian Cohen
Paintings copyright © 2016 by Rosemary Hartounian Cohen

ALL RIGHTS RESERVED under International and Pan-American Copyright Conventions. Except for brief quotation in reviews or articles, no parts of this book may be reproduced by any means. Inquiries should be addressed to the author and publisher.

Library of Congress Cataloging-in-Publication Data:
Cohen, Rosemary H. - author and illustrator
ISBN:978-0-9969741-0-3
UPC # 795808-41822

1. Fairy Tale
2. Science Fiction
3. Religion & Spirituality
4. Color
5. Color in Art
6. Basic Guide of Mixing Colors

pp: 98

The Cover Design and all the illustrations are painted on silk by: Rosemary Hartounian Cohen
Photography of art works: Joe Shalmoni
Book Cover & Interior Design by: Elia B. Cohen & Lidia Suvarova

Contact the author at: rosemary@atelierdeparis.com

Published by Lico Publishing
1541 South Robertson Boulevard
Los Angeles, CA 90035

Printed in the Republic of China

BERESHIT – Genesis I

Creation – The Fifth Day

20. And God said: "Let the waters swarm with swarms of living creatures, and let fowl fly above the earth in the open firmament of heaven."

21. And God created the great sea-monsters and every living creature that creepeth, wherewith the waters swarmed, after its kind, and every winged fowl after its kind: and God saw that it was good.

22. And God blessed them, saying: "Be fruitful, and multiply, and fill the waters in the seas, and let fowl multiply in the earth. There was evening and there was morning, a fifth day."

❖

BERESHIT – Genesis II

1. And the heavens and the earth were finished, and all the host of them.

2. And on the seventh day, God finished His work, which He had made: and He rested on the seventh day from all His work, which He had made.

3. And God blessed the seventh day, and hallowed it: because, that in it, He rested from all his work, which God in creating had made.

---

* Genesis – Bereshit: Chapter I, verses 20, 21, 22, 23
* Genesis – Bereshit: Chapter II, verses 1, 2, 3
* The Pentateuch and Haftorahs, edited by Dr. J. H. Hertz, C.H., London, Soncino Press, second edition, 1965

Learn How to Mix Colors
from
Angel Liana

After the completion of the creations, life continued growing and multiplying on earth and in heaven. And God expected that humans would become His partners in the creation and improve and beautify the earth with the hidden talents that He has given to every creature.

"Shabbat,"* the seventh day, is a gift given to everyone in order to rest one day a week. Everyone works hard for six days of the week; therefore, to rest one day a week is a blessing.

The angels also respect Shabbat; they sing together honoring God's glory. It is known that the angels have beautiful and sweet voices, and this is the reason that "angelic voice" has entered in our vocabulary.

The angels also talk together and share their thoughts on how to use their knowledge and talents in order to add to the already existing beauty in the world. This, in turn, helps to glorify creation.

---

* Shabbat: We read in Bereshit – the Creation: God worked for six days, and on the seventh day, Shabbat, He rested and ordered that we do the same: "Remember the Shabbat day, to keep it holy." [Exodus 20:8]

Although we all believe in the same unique God, unfortunately, Christian and Muslim authorities changed God's words after many centuries. Shabbat, which was celebrated on Saturday, changed to Sunday for the Christians, and Muslims chose Friday as their Shabbat.

I believe this change created many conflicts in the world. I look forward to the day when we will all celebrate Shabbat on the same day so everyone will pray and rest at the same time. I am sure that this change, by itself, will create harmony among different people, similar to the color wheel, and finally, peace will be established for everyone and on earth.

Book One
Angel Liana

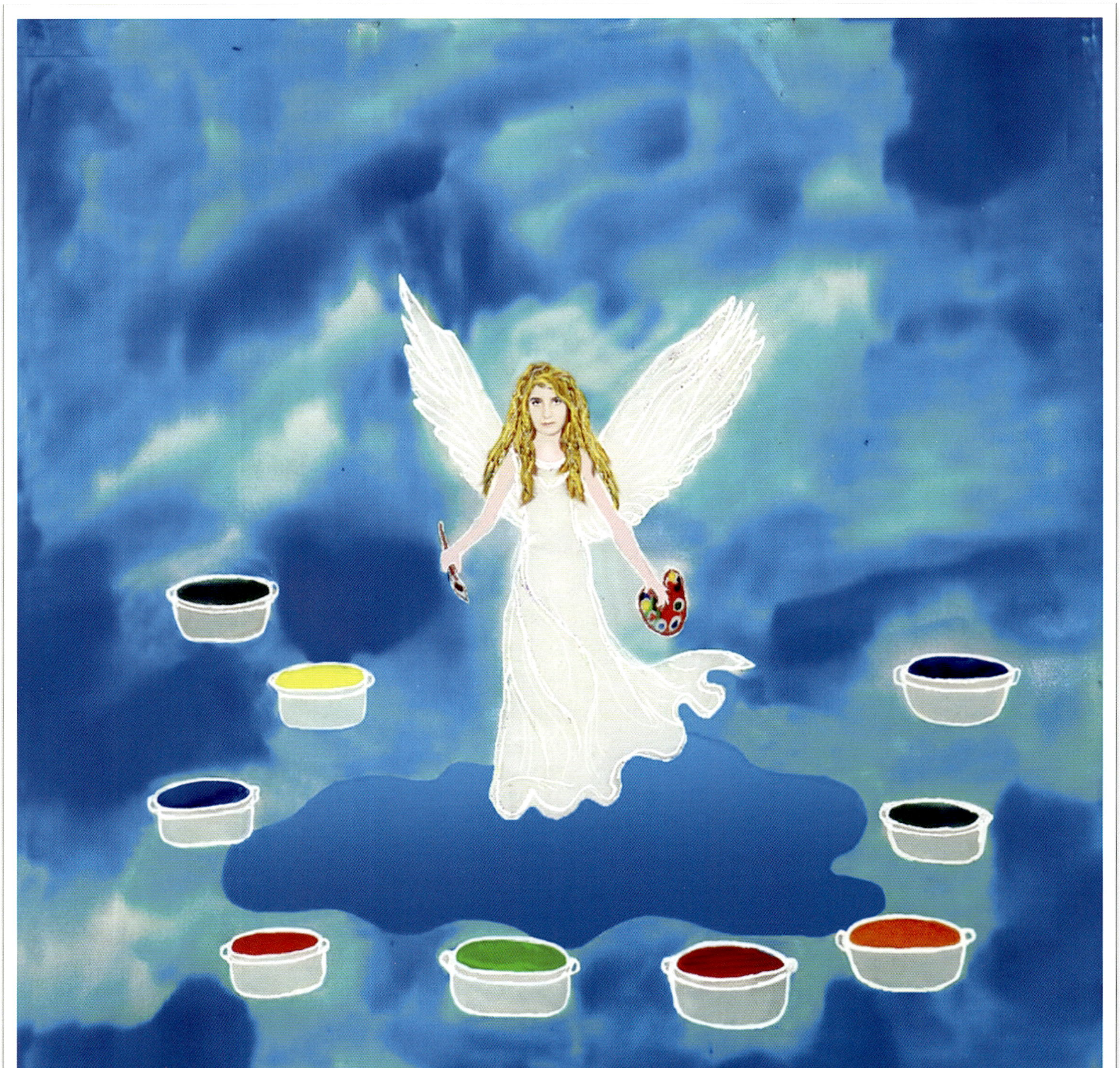

Liana, a young and beautiful angel, was always ready to help and use her talents when needed. Like all the angels, she had also an "angelic voice."

Angel Liana was also very talented in the arts, with a specialty in colors.

She knew how to mix the three primary colors together and create additional ones in beautiful shades. Any angel who had a problem in mixing colors would always ask Angel Liana's advice.

One day Angel Liana was looking at the earth, admiring the azure blue surface of the waters and praising God for the beauty that He had created.

She saw the water swarm with moving creatures full of life, but most of them looked transparent. From afar, she could see sparkling fish in the water. Suddenly, the rain fell from the heavens onto the earth. As it stopped raining, the sun took back its glory and its rays created a colorful rainbow in the sky.

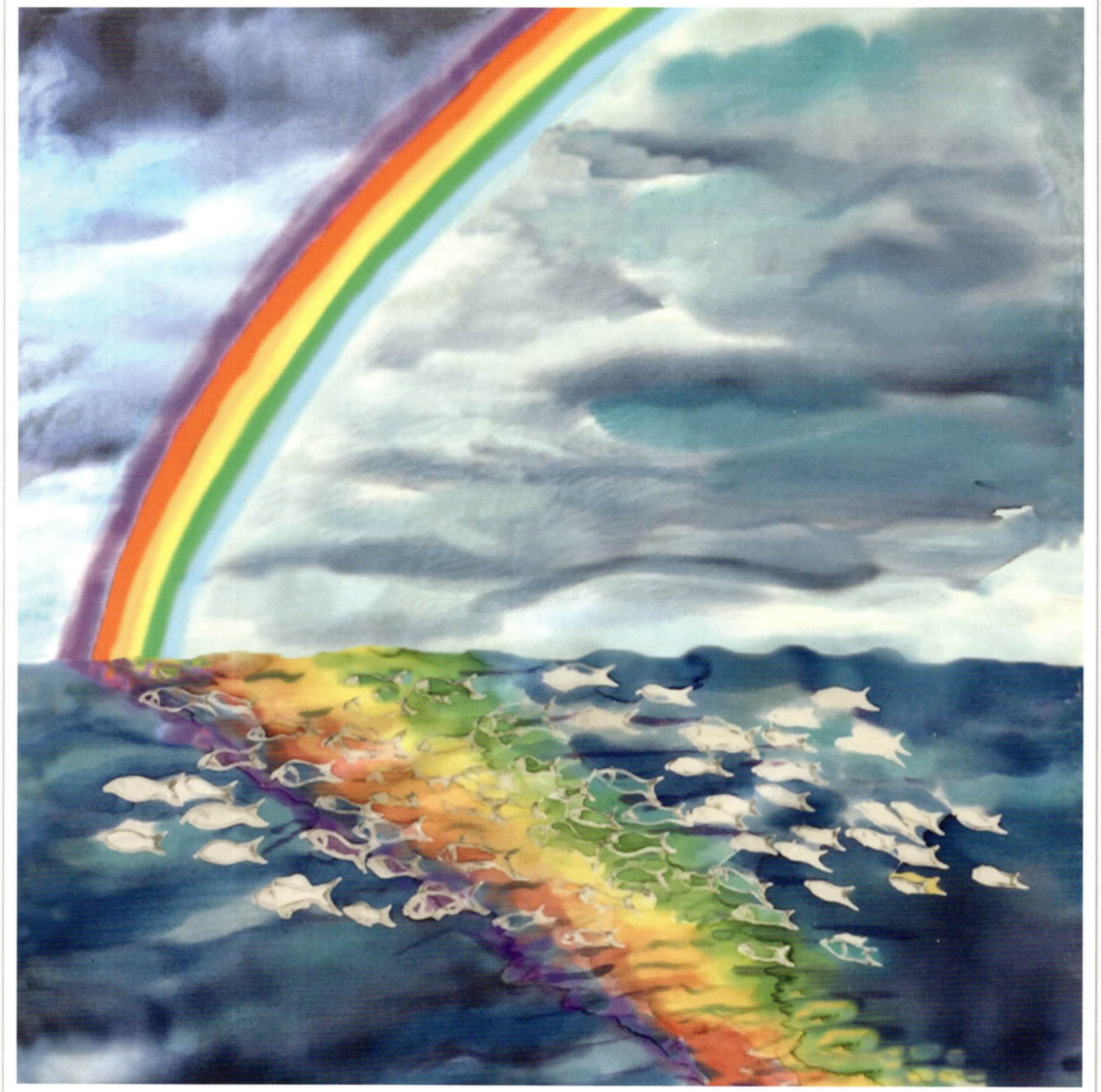

The colors of the rainbow reflected on the surface of the water and the transparent fish of many different sizes were tinted by the rainbow shades. So the water became colorful. Some fish turned to red or yellow; others turned to blue, violet, and green colors. But as the rainbow faded and disappeared, so did the colors on the fish and the surface of the water.

At that exact moment, Angel Liana heard a call and the message was: "Wouldn't it be nice if the colors on the fish were permanent?"

She cried out, excited: "Oh, yes, yes! Can I be of help somehow?"

Angel Liana had learned and knew that there were only three primary colors. Some use yellow, red, and blue. Others use yellow, magenta, and cyan.

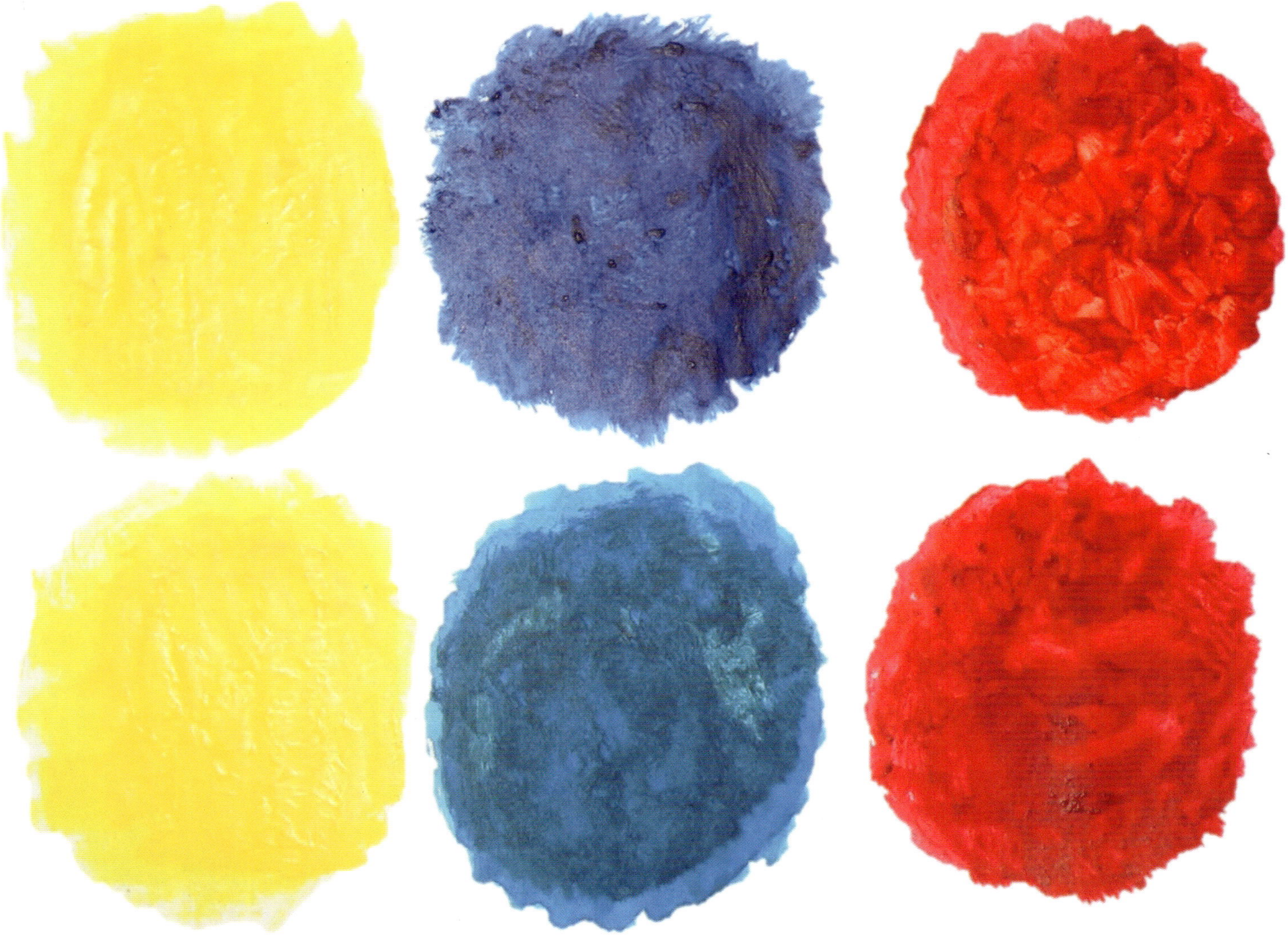

The primary colors: Red, Yellow, Blue
or
Magenta, Yellow, Cyan,

We will use yellow, red, and blue since many people recognize it easier. We will also use yellow, magenta, and cyan so that you will be able to see the difference.

Angel Liana first learned to mix colors. She found that by mixing an equal amount of the two primary colors, she could create a secondary color.

red + yellow = orange red + blue = violet blue + yellow = green

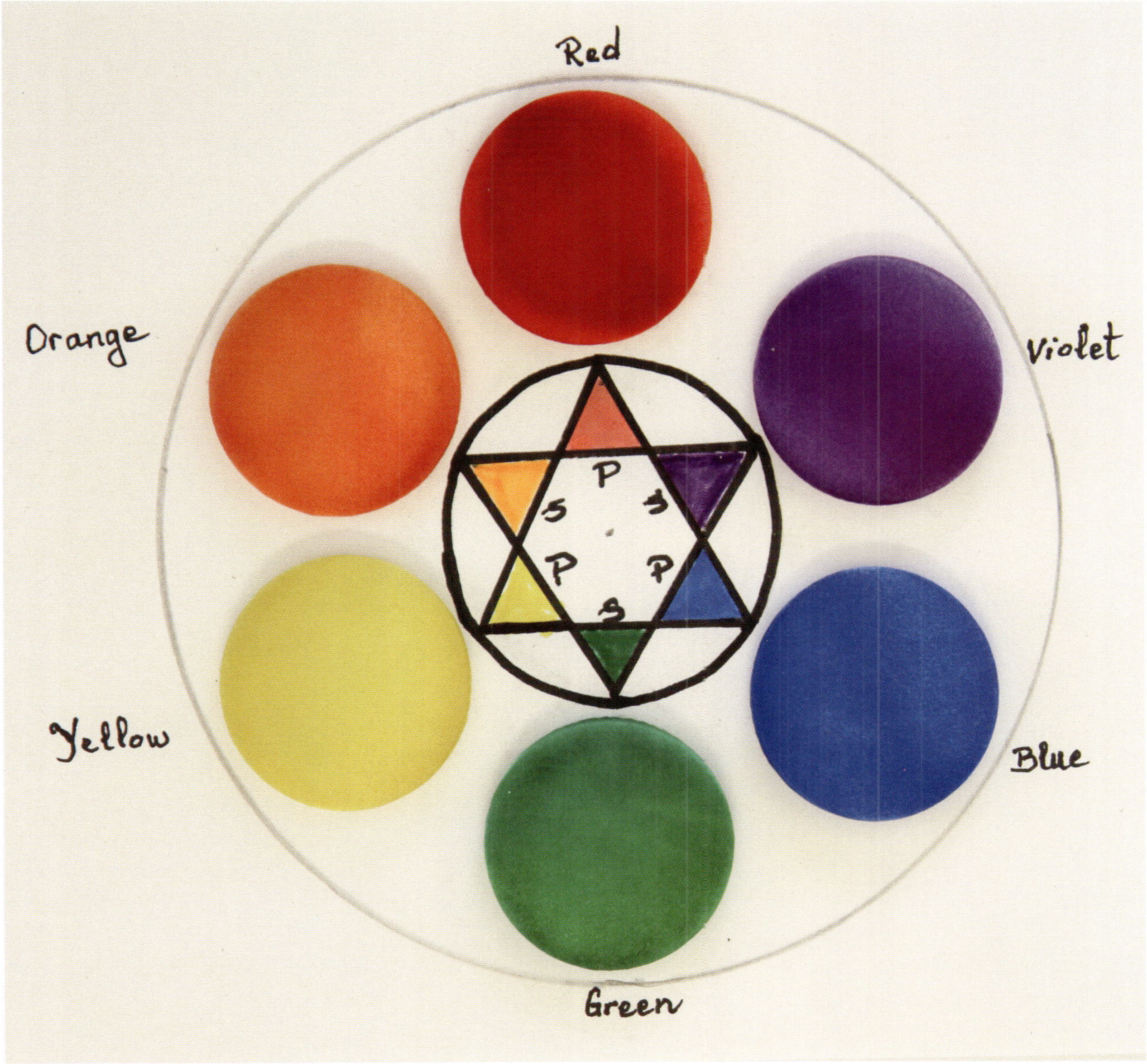

Primary and secondary colors

Mixing the primary colors, results: secondary colors and by mixing the secondary colors together results the complementary colors.

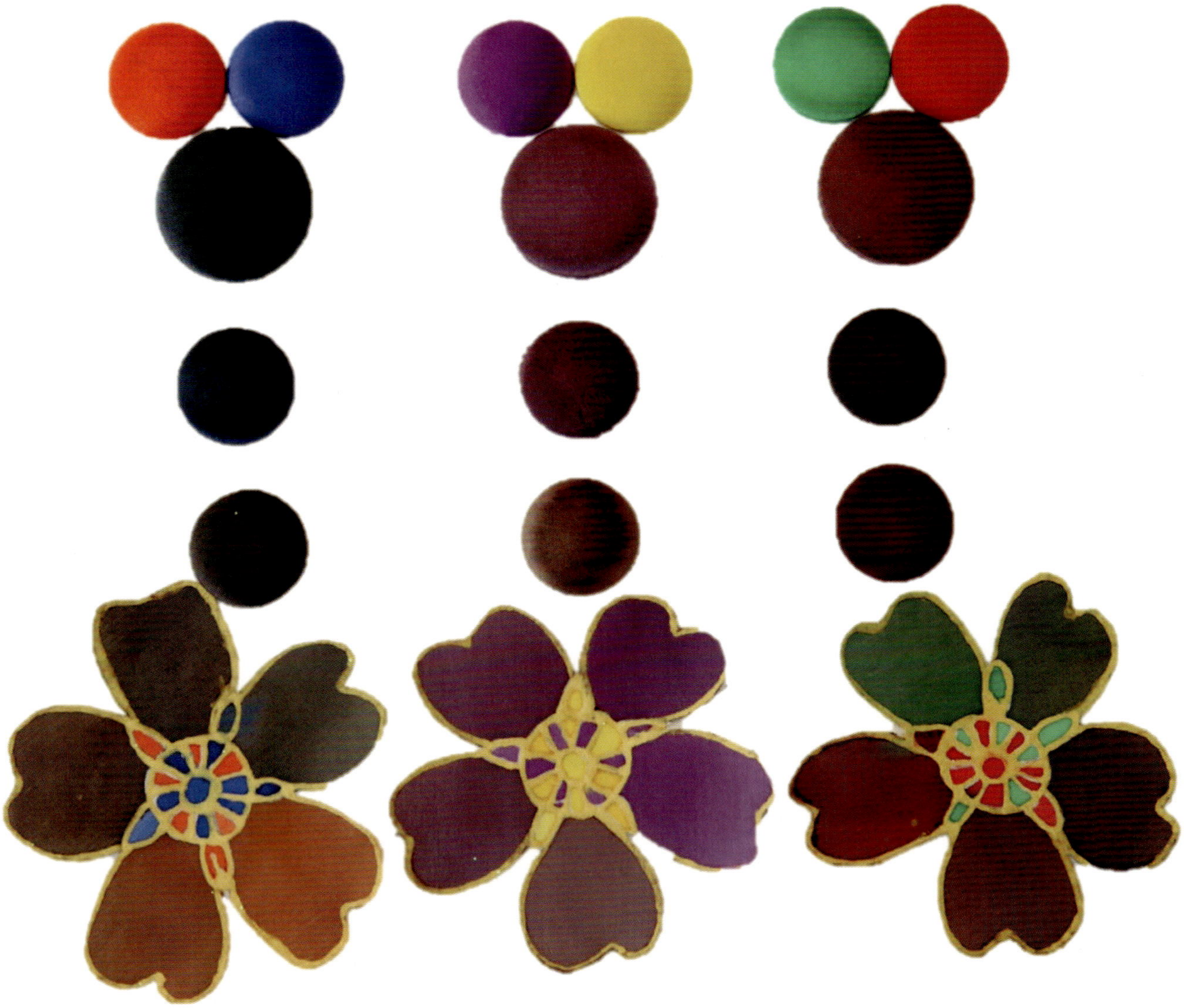

2 blue + 2 orange	2 violet + 2 yellow	2 green + 2 red
6 blue + 3 orange	6 violet + 3 yellow	6 green + 3 red
3 blue + 3 orange	3 violet + 6 yellow	3 green + 6 red

The flowers petal colors are made out of the same colors combination but with different measures:

2+2 4+1 6+1 24+1 36+1

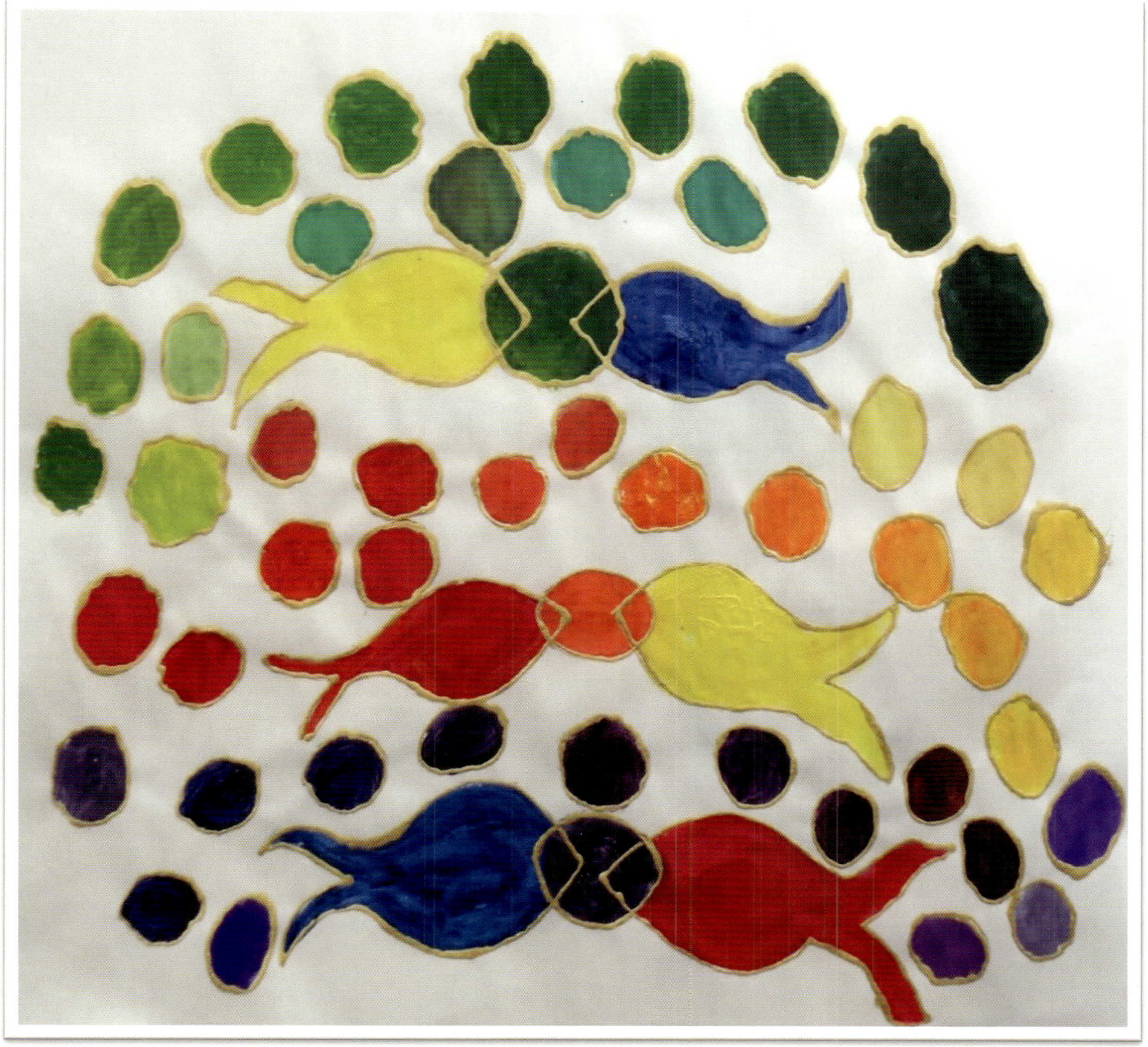

By mixing the three primary colors of Yellow, Red and Blue, the secondary colors are obtained which are orange, green and violet.

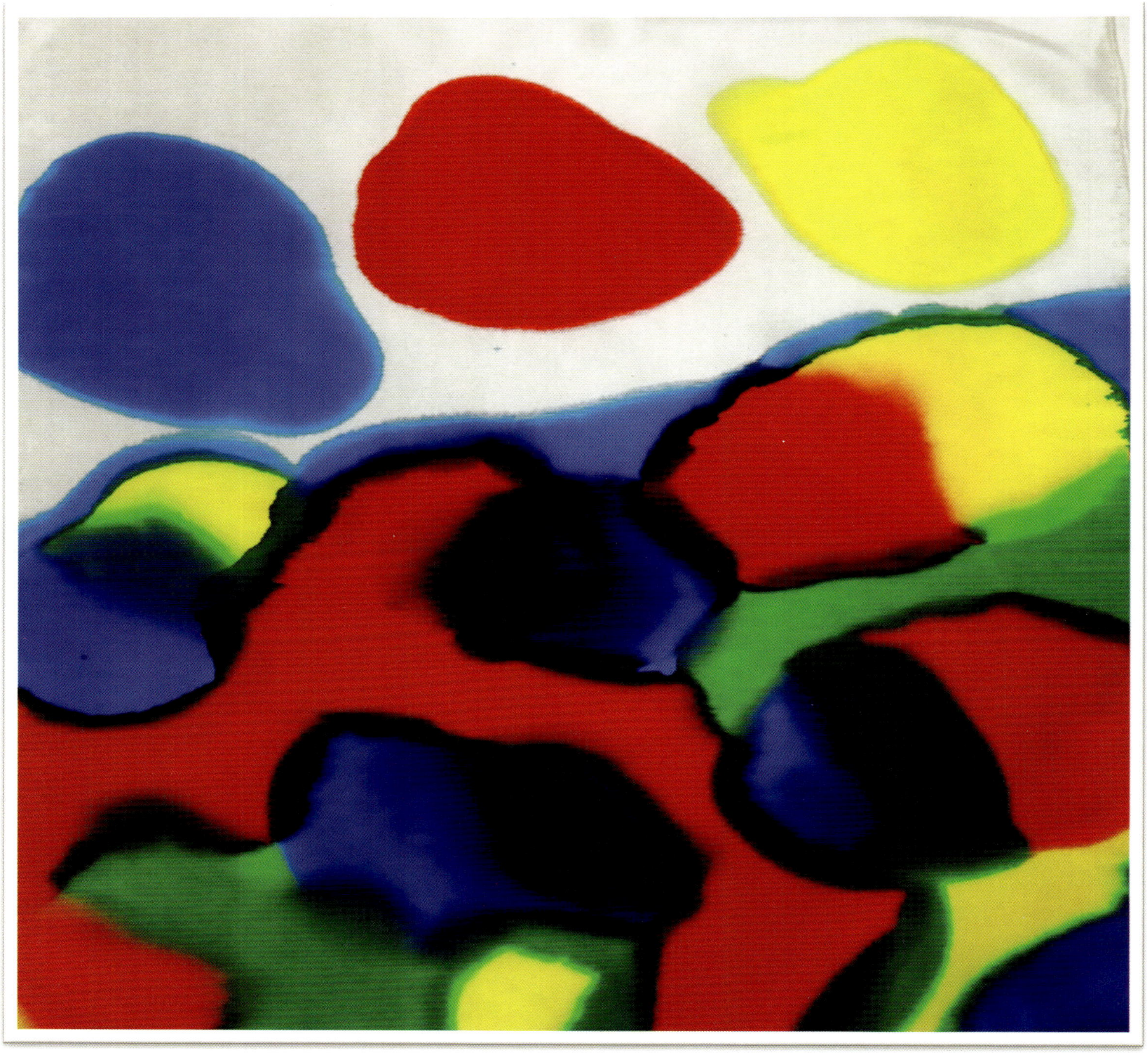

Artistic abstract painting is obtained by mixing the three primary and as you put them side by side they touch each other and the secondary colors of orange, violet, and green appear between them.

As time passed, she learned how to mix the secondary colors together and obtained many additional new ones. She was surprised to discover that, in a day, she was able to make hundreds of different shades of colors, just by mixing the three primary colors with the secondary colors. This process creates the complementary colors, which are:

red + green   violet + yellow   blue + orange

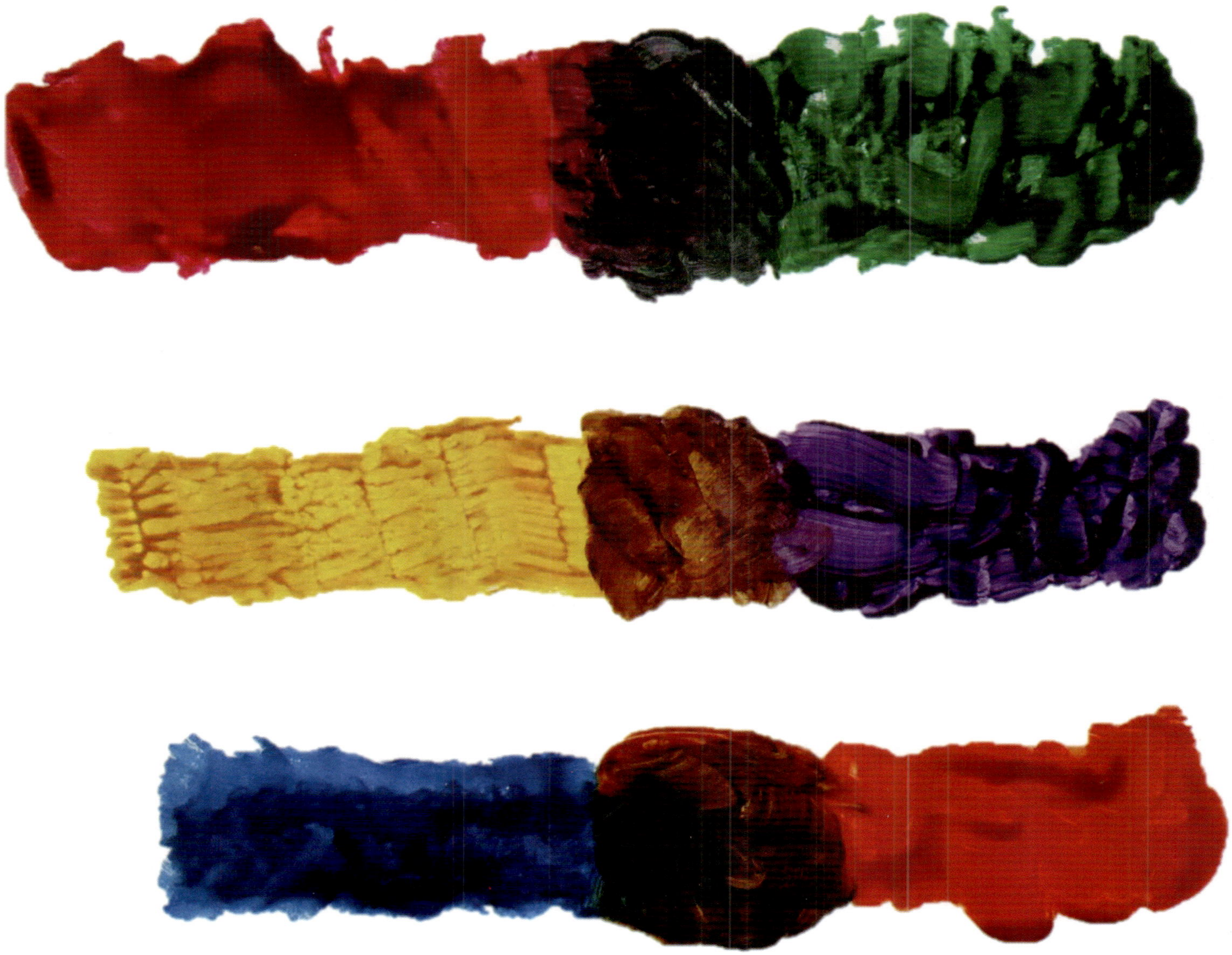

Can you help Angel Liana find additional shades of colors?

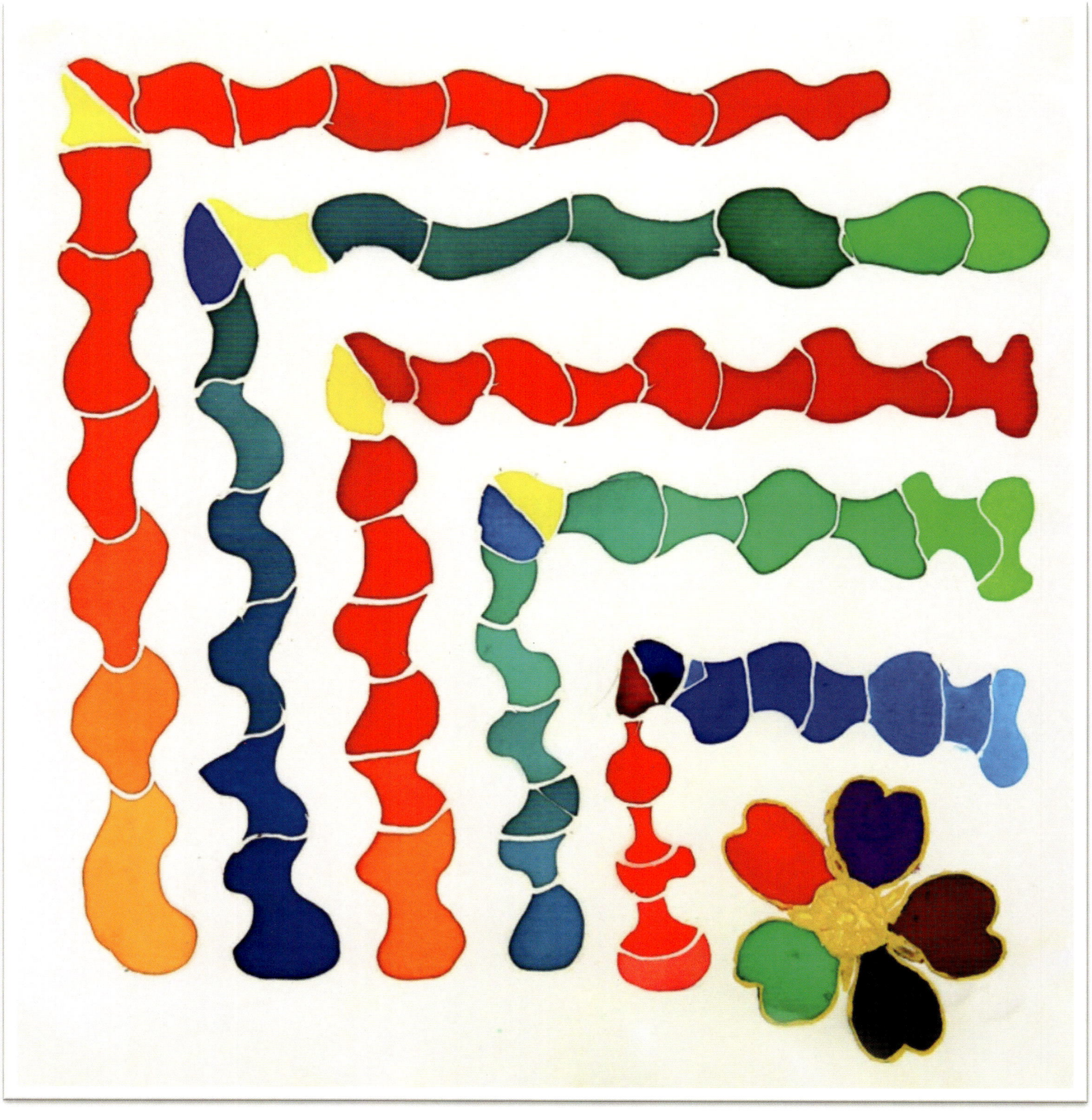

In this picture we have used the two colors that are in each corners, (Like outer one): Yellow and Red are used in these two columns, mixing:

Horizontal: 1 drop Yellow +1 drop Red, 2 drop Yellow + 1 drop Red, 4Y+1R, 6 Y+1R, 24Y+1R, 36Y+1R

Vertical: Red+ Yellow, the Yellow will stay one drop and Red will follow the same measure as in A from one drop to 36 drops

This formula will continue on each line:
2nd line with Yellow and Blue
3rd line with Magenta and Yellow
4th line Yellow and Cyan
5th line is the result of adding water to the Cyan and Magenta colors, it shows the lighter "pastel" colors obtained.

The flower shows the three secondary colors of Green, Violet and Orange with two mixed of three different colors resulting: Brown and Black.

Usually, the color-mixing chart is always shown in the shape of a circle, known as a color wheel. Probably this name is given because the primary colors follow each other. The circle goes round and round and does not end, so the colors follow and mix with each other and create new colors.

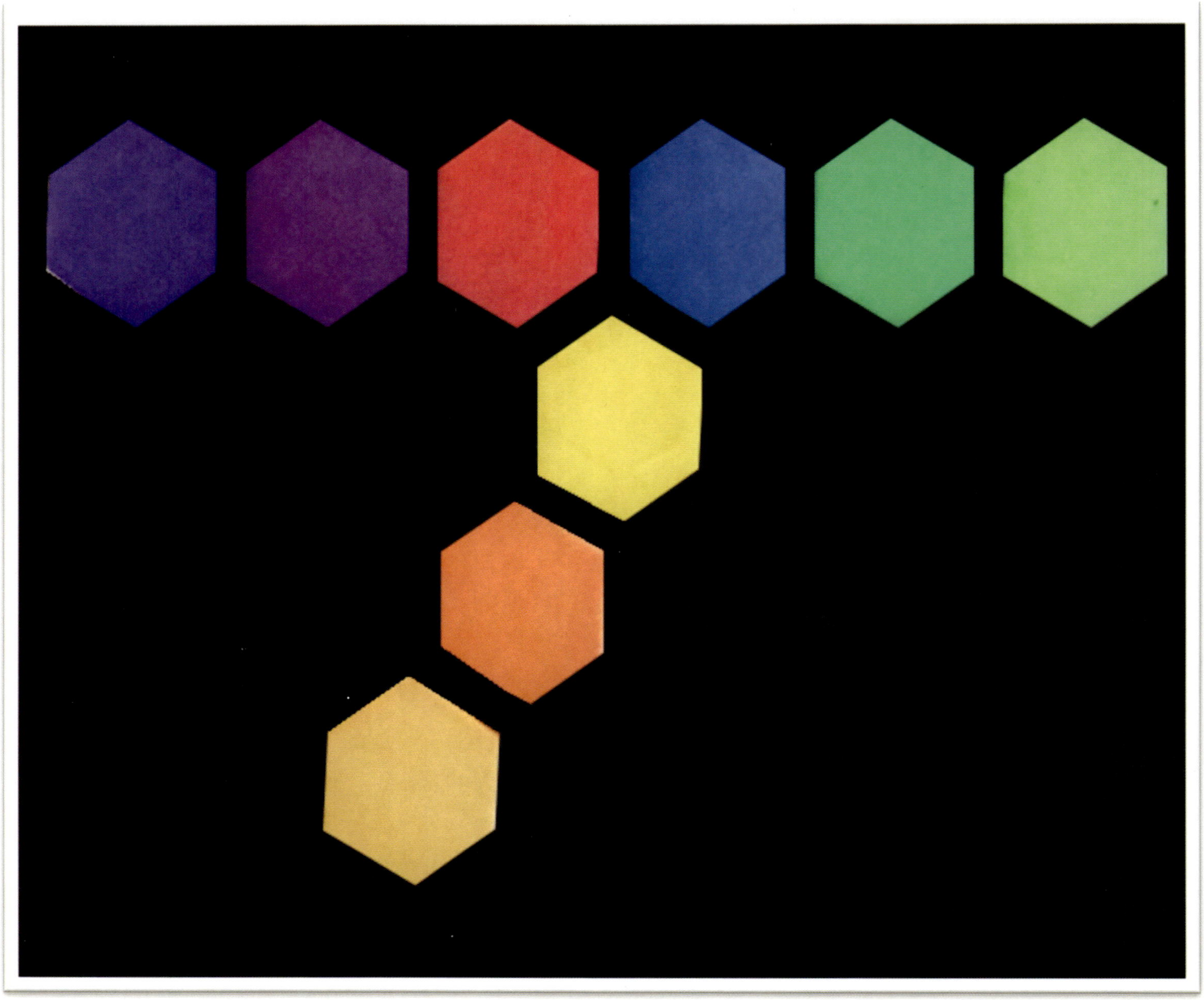

Be creative and use all kinds of shapes that will show the primary colors.

Remember: Think of the color wheel as a circle of good friends holding hands together. They have different colors, but all of them stay together in harmony.

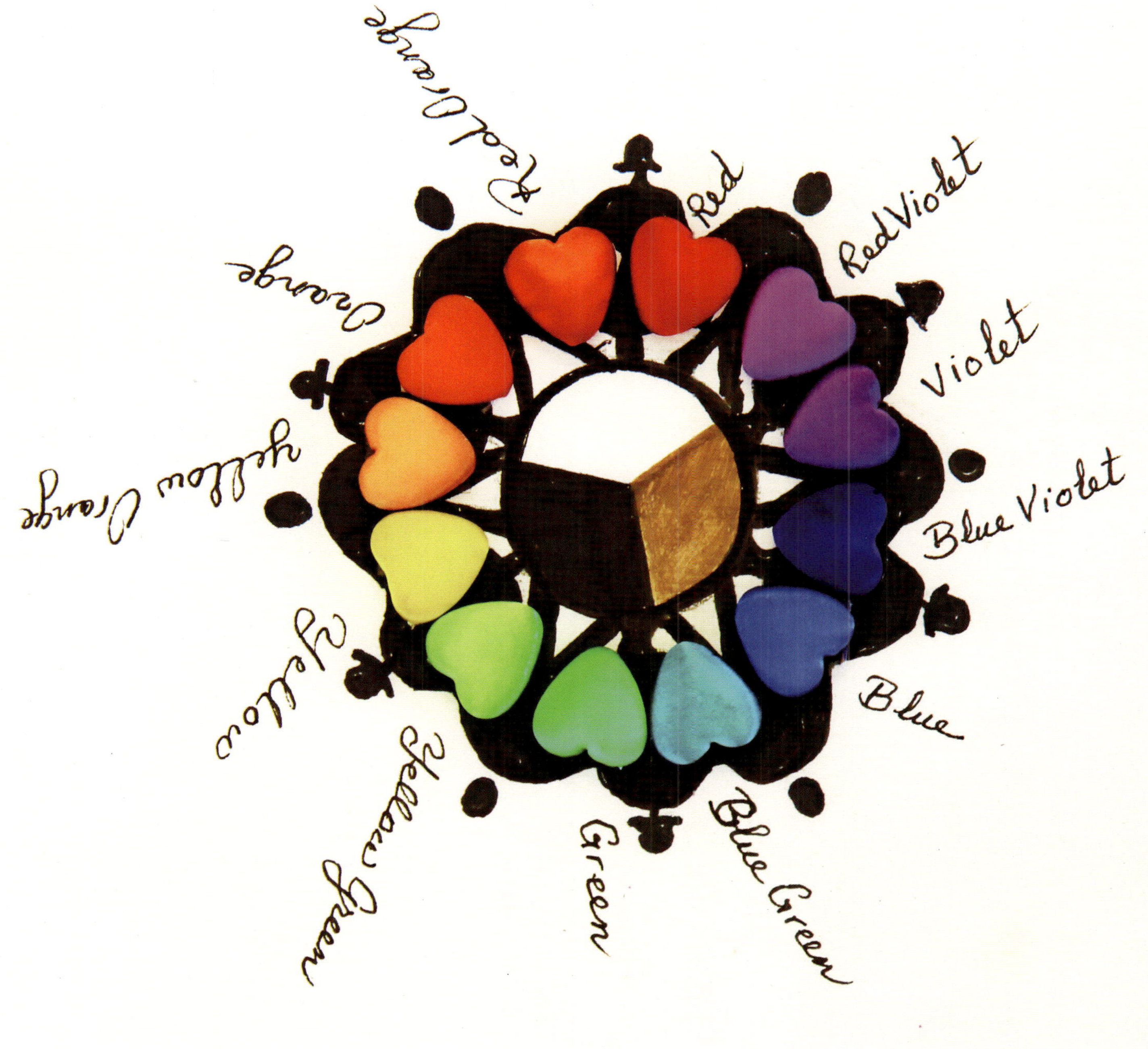

For example, if you pull any color, the next one nearby will follow too. Again, like holding hands, if they hold hard and pull one of them, the next will follow. If you pull the red side, which is close to yellow, the yellow will stretch toward the red. Therefore, you will obtain all orange shades between these two colors.

The same is true for the blue and yellow colors. If you pull the blue toward the yellow, the yellow will stretch and come to help the blue, and all the green shades will appear between them. And, finally, this is also true with blue and red, where all shades of violet and purple will appear between them.

red + yellow   yellow + blue   blue + red

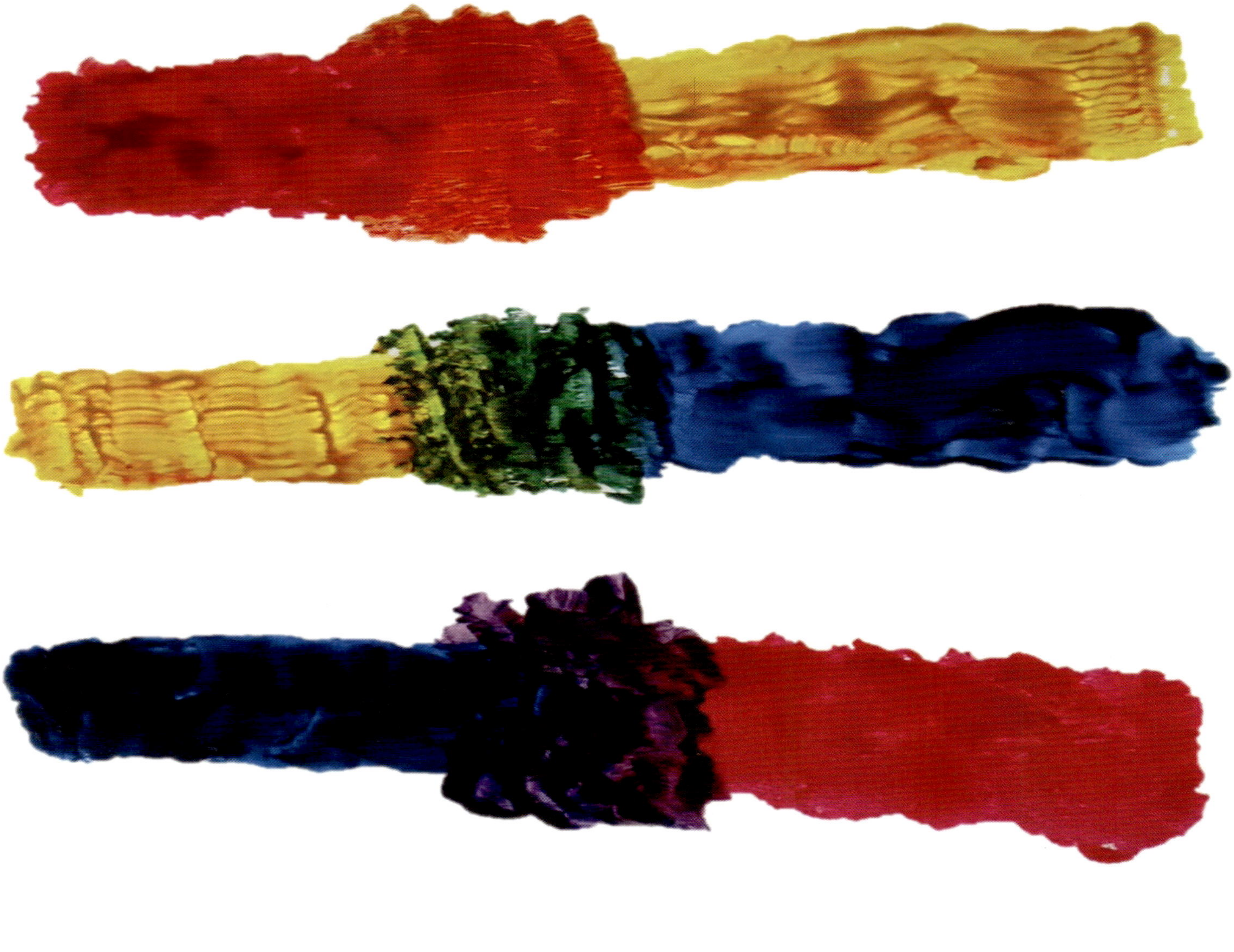

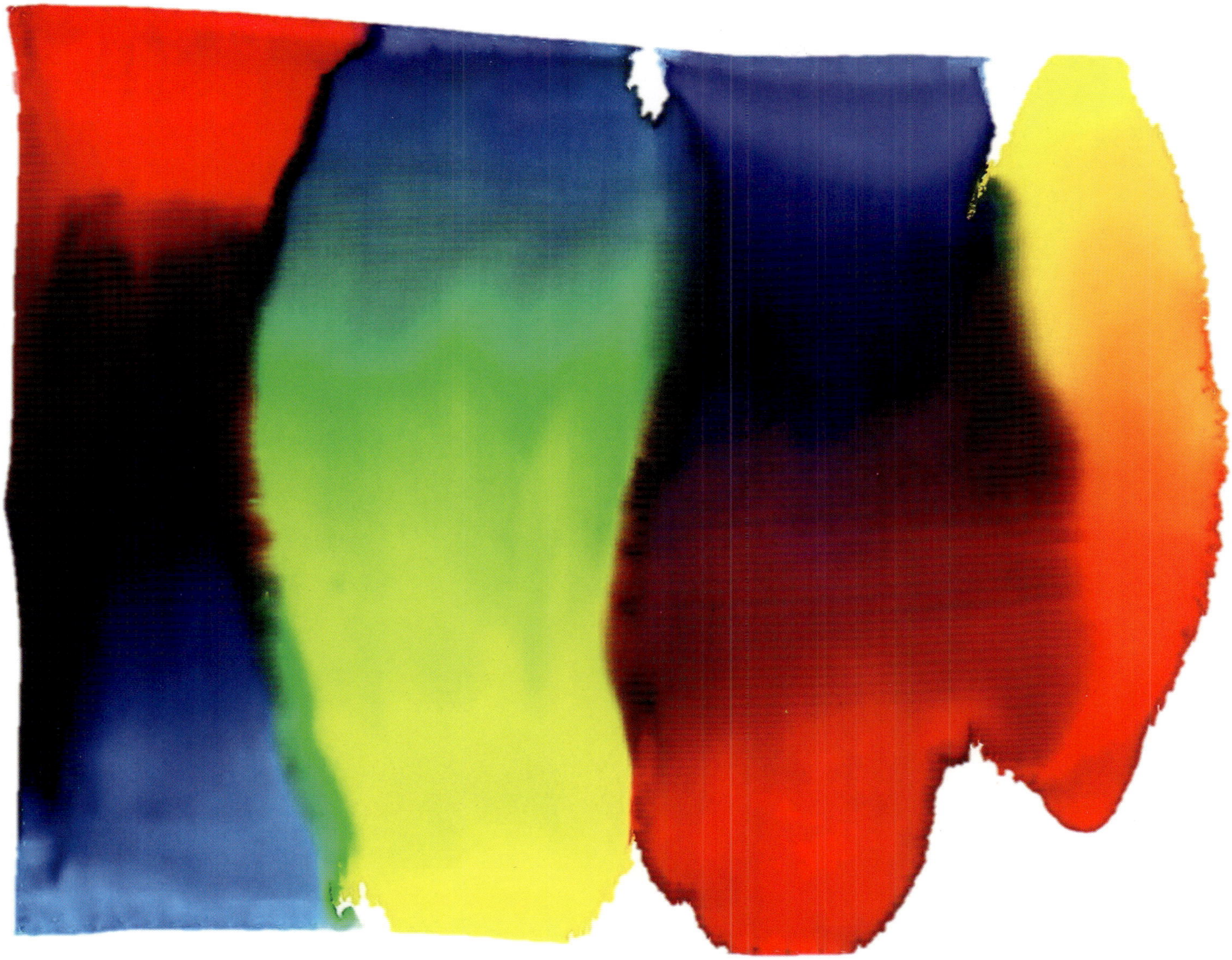

We have used the three primary colors on each side of the line from upper:
Yellow – red, blue – red, cyan-yellow, magenta and cyan
We have obtained all the different shades in between the two primary colors and even more colors between each line that have touched each other.

Note: In order to obtain a true formula, you should always use one brush for each color. For example, if the yellow brush is used for red or blue colors, you can never obtain a pure yellow with that brush even if you wash it with baby shampoo and water.

In this picture we can see the primary colors on each side and in the middle we can see the secondary colors appear in different shades.

The four top colors Turquoise & yellow to the left, magenta & blue to the right represent the dominating color in the mixture.

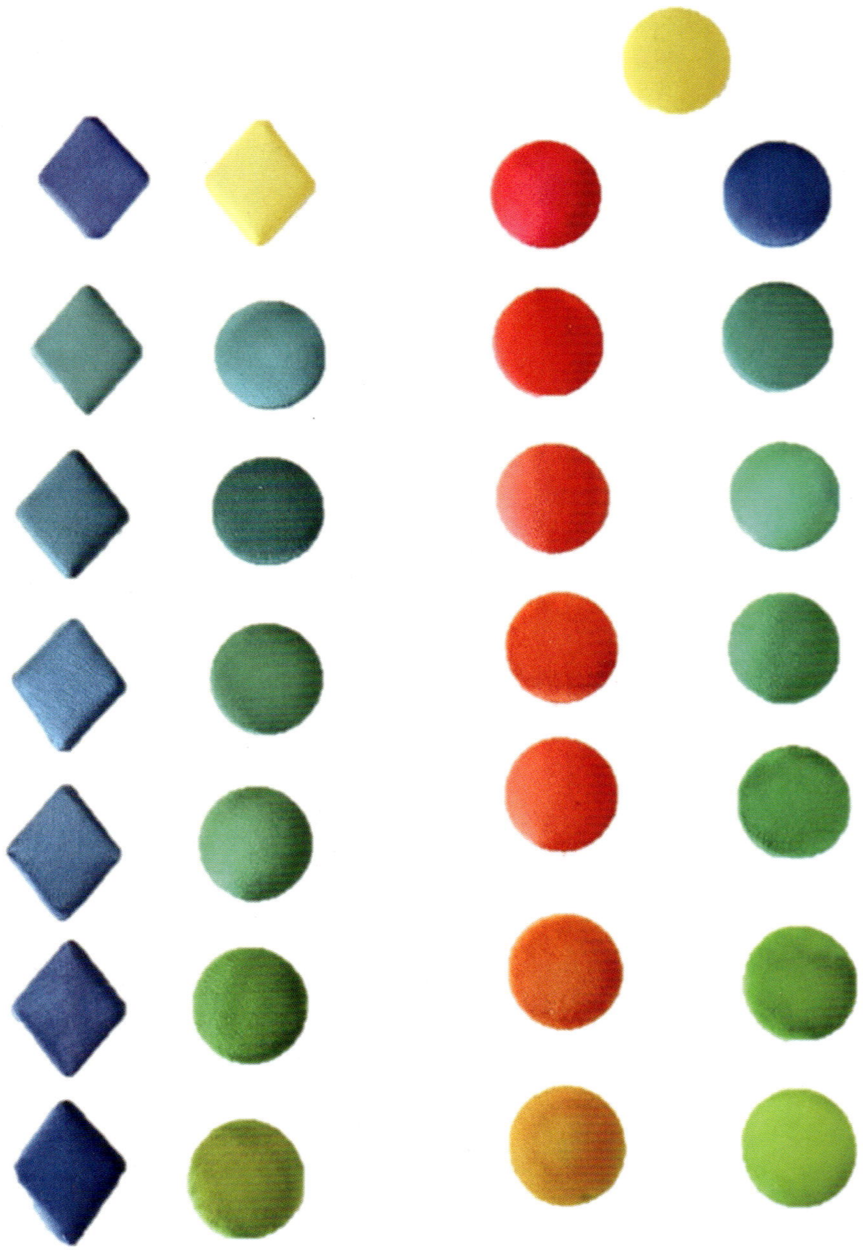

The columns:

1. Blue dominating to only one drop of yellow
2. Yellow dominating to only one drop of blue
3. Magenta dominating to one drop of yellow
4. Cyan dominating to one drop of yellow

On the following chart there are four columns that are mixed as the following:

1st column left:

1 drop blue to 1 drop of yellow — and the result is dark green.

2 drops of blue to 1 drop of yellow.

4 drops of blue to one drop of yellow.

6 drops and then 24 and 36 drops of blue to one drop of yellow on each mixture

In the second column, Angel Liana repeats this formula, using the same amount of drops with blue and yellow. Then the next column is the same amount of drops to the mixture of magenta and yellow. In the last column, she mixes the cyan with yellow, and in this last mixture the results will show different shades of green.

Some Formulas

The next picture shows the basic practice for color mixing. In the first column, Angel Liana has used different drops of yellow to only one drop of red in each mixture to obtain orange shades reaching the gold color, as follows:

With Primary Color: YELLOW

Quantity of Yellow	Quantity of Red	Result Obtained
1 yellow	1 red	orange
2 yellow	1 red	
4 yellow	1 red	
6 yellow	1 red	
24 yellow	1 red	
36 yellow	1 red	gold

With Primary Color: RED

Quantity of Red	Quantity of Yellow	Result Obtained
1 red	1 yellow	orange
2 red	1 yellow	
4 red	1 yellow	
6 red	1 yellow	
24 red	1 yellow	
36 red	1 yellow	dark red

Continue mixing your formula as much as you wish.
You can also try other mixing games, like changing the numbers to:
2 yellow + 4 red
6 red + 2 yellow
Play with all numbers and the two colors.

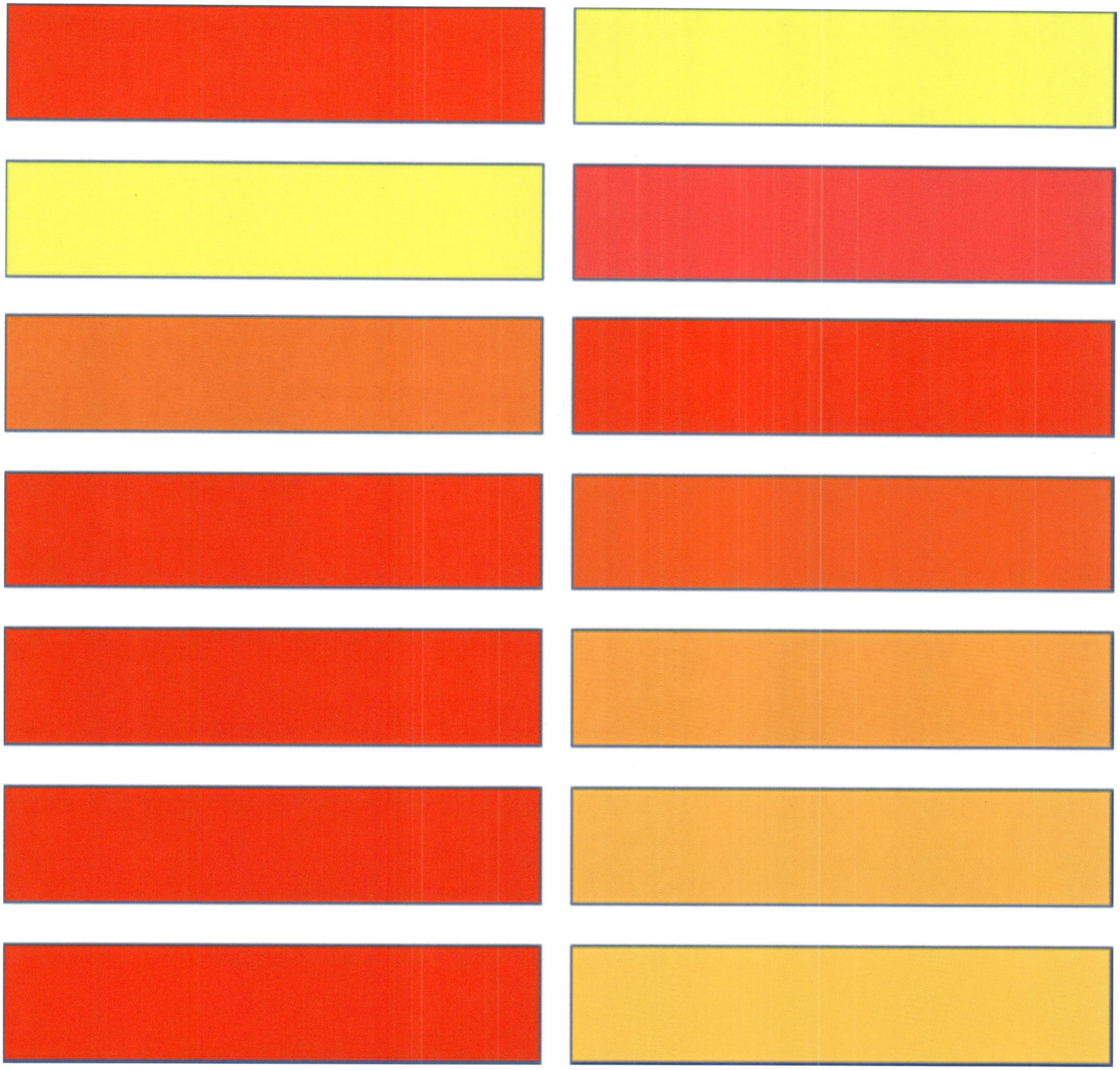

In the first row, when yellow is added to the red, the colors change in each step. But in the second column we realize that as we add more red to a drop of yellow colors do not change much.

Let Angel Liana know if you have been able to find how to make brown and black colors. I will give you one tip: you have to mix three colors together. Find how many drops of each color you have to use in order to obtain brown and black colors. Write down the formula in the parentheses.

Blue (------) + yellow (-----) + red (-----) = Brown

Blue (------) + yellow (-----) + red (-----) = Black

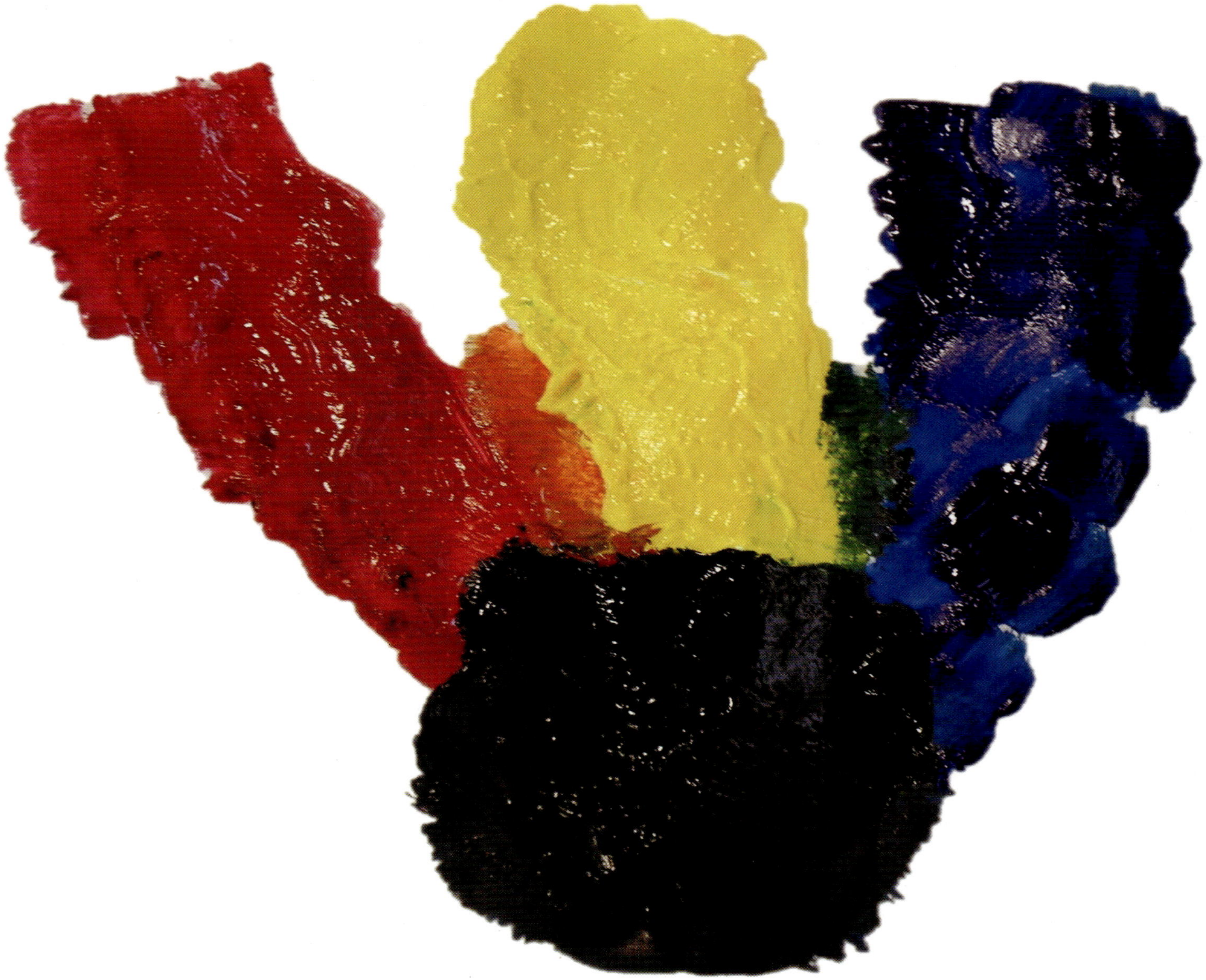

Finally, Angel Liana was ordered to go down to the ocean one day and teach the fish the art of mixing colors.

The angels were always told that God created the earth and heavens, but all men and women are also created in His image. Therefore, they have the necessary knowledge and talent in order to improve and beautify the continuation of the creation the best way they can.

Of course, the angels are also created to help the humans and creatures on earth when they are called for.

To accomplish her mission, Angel Liana received a beautiful magic brush that had a long shiny handle.

The handle was divided into three equal parts. Angel Liana went to the source where they keep the concentrated colors. These colors are very strong, shiny, soft, and beautiful. The colors are so concentrated that, with just a tiny drop, she could paint a lot of large projects and cover many surfaces. She filled each section with the concentrated primary colors of **Yellow**, **Red**, and **Blue**.

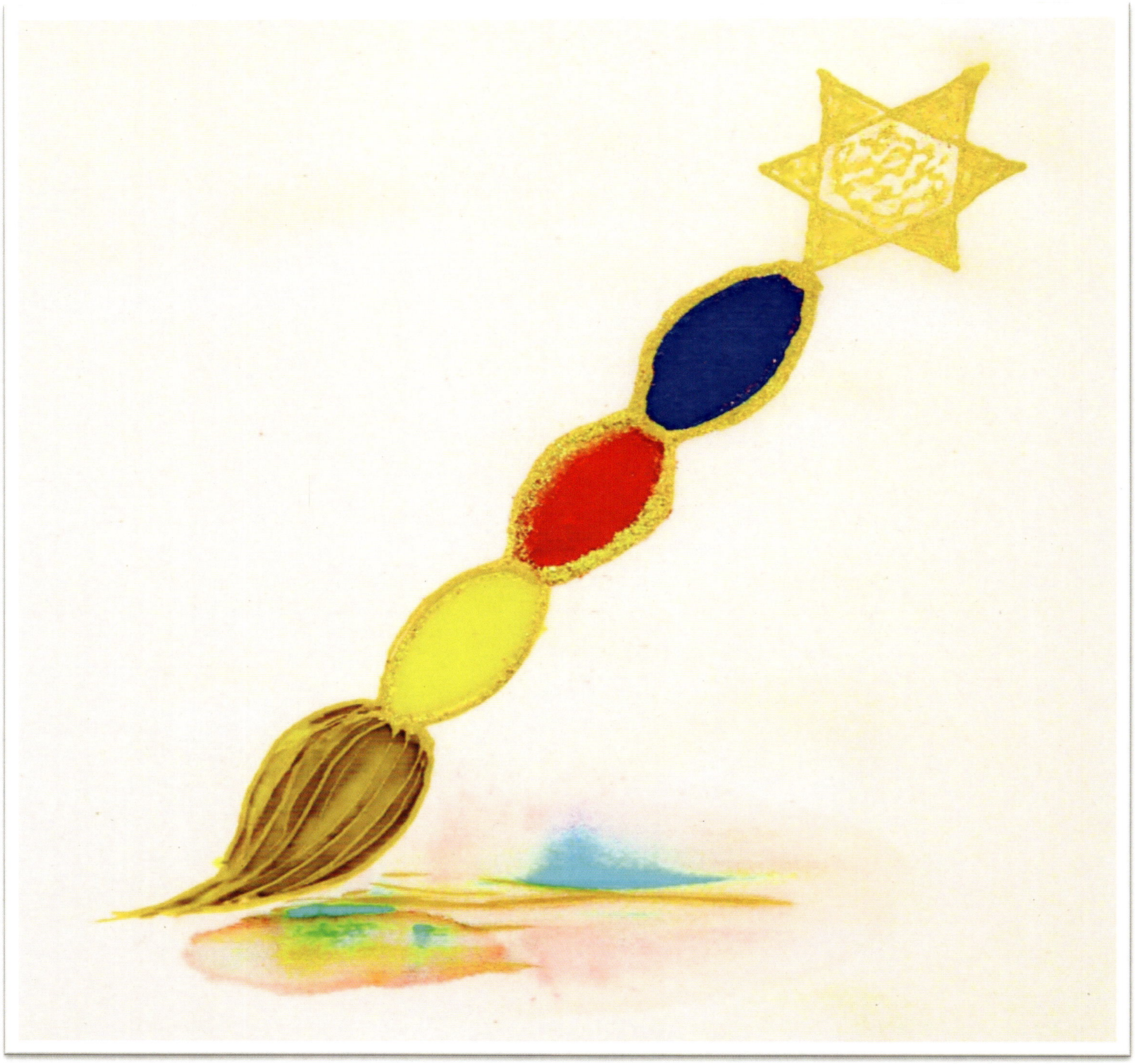

Liana's magic brush

At one end of the brush, very soft angels' hair was gathered together to form the tip. With this tip, she had the proper tool in order to mix colors, as well as use it for painting.

At the end of the handle sat a glittering golden star. She was told that the star had an amazing magical power. When she needed something or was in difficulty, she could gently strike the star and receive additional help.

For example, when she was going to enter the water, if she hit the star once on her wings, they would turn into fins to help her swim in the water. If she tapped the brush twice on her feet, her two legs would turn into a mermaid's tail so that she could swim faster and deeper in the water.

But she was going to need large mixing cups in order to prepare colors. By hitting on the empty shells three times, the little shells would turn into large containers and buckets in order to mix and store colors.

Angel Liana received the blessings and the permission for the time that she needed to accomplish her task. She said goodbye to everyone and headed down toward earth. She enjoyed the flight by sometimes holding the magic brush with her two hands like a steering wheel, and soon she descended toward the surface of the water.

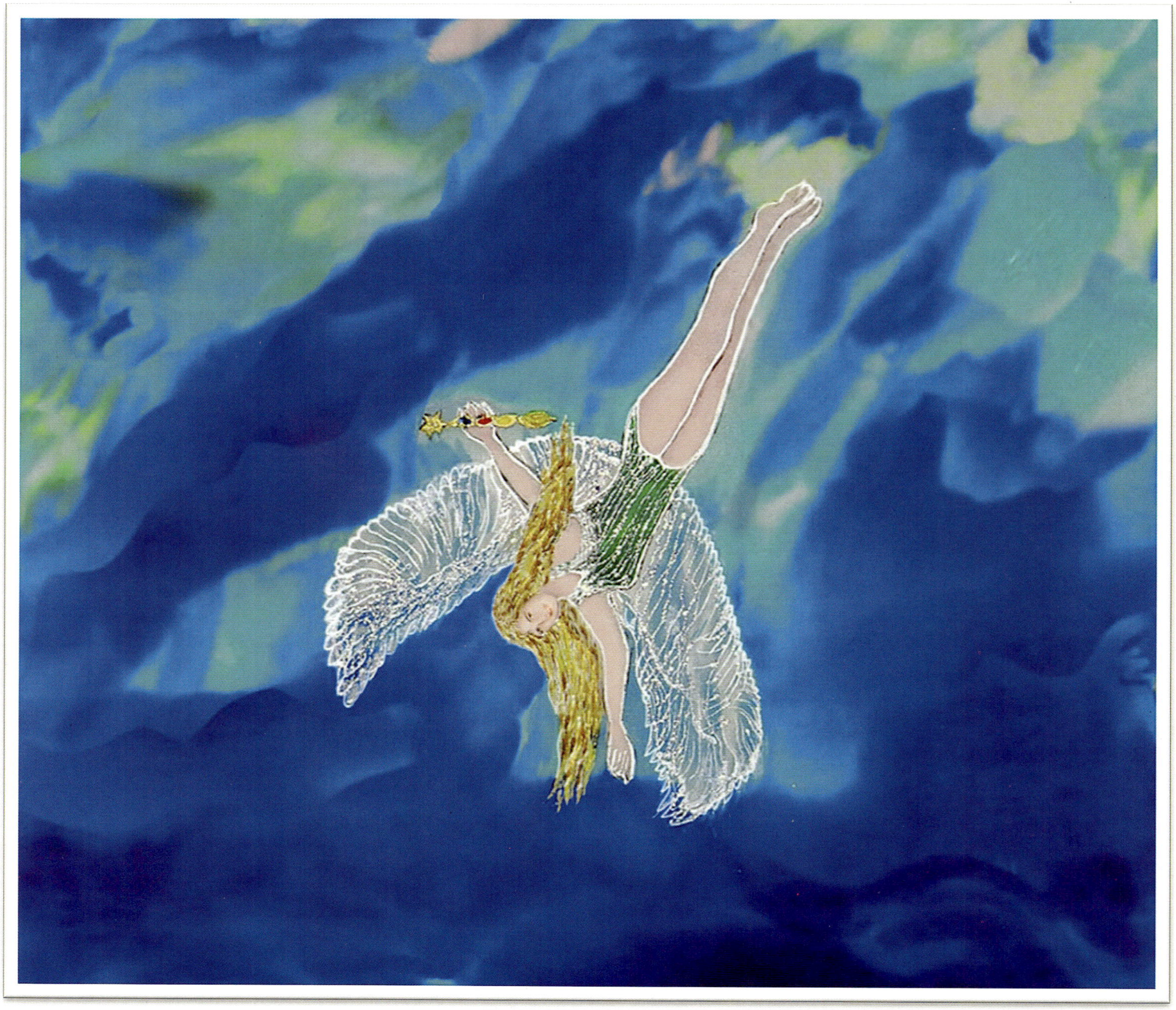

As Angel Liana approached the surface of the water, she hit the magic brush once on her wings and they immediately turned into two large fins.

Then Angel Liana hit the brush twice on her legs and they turned into caudal peduncles, the narrow part of a fish's body where the tail fin is attached.

Here is what the caudal peduncle of a fish looks like:

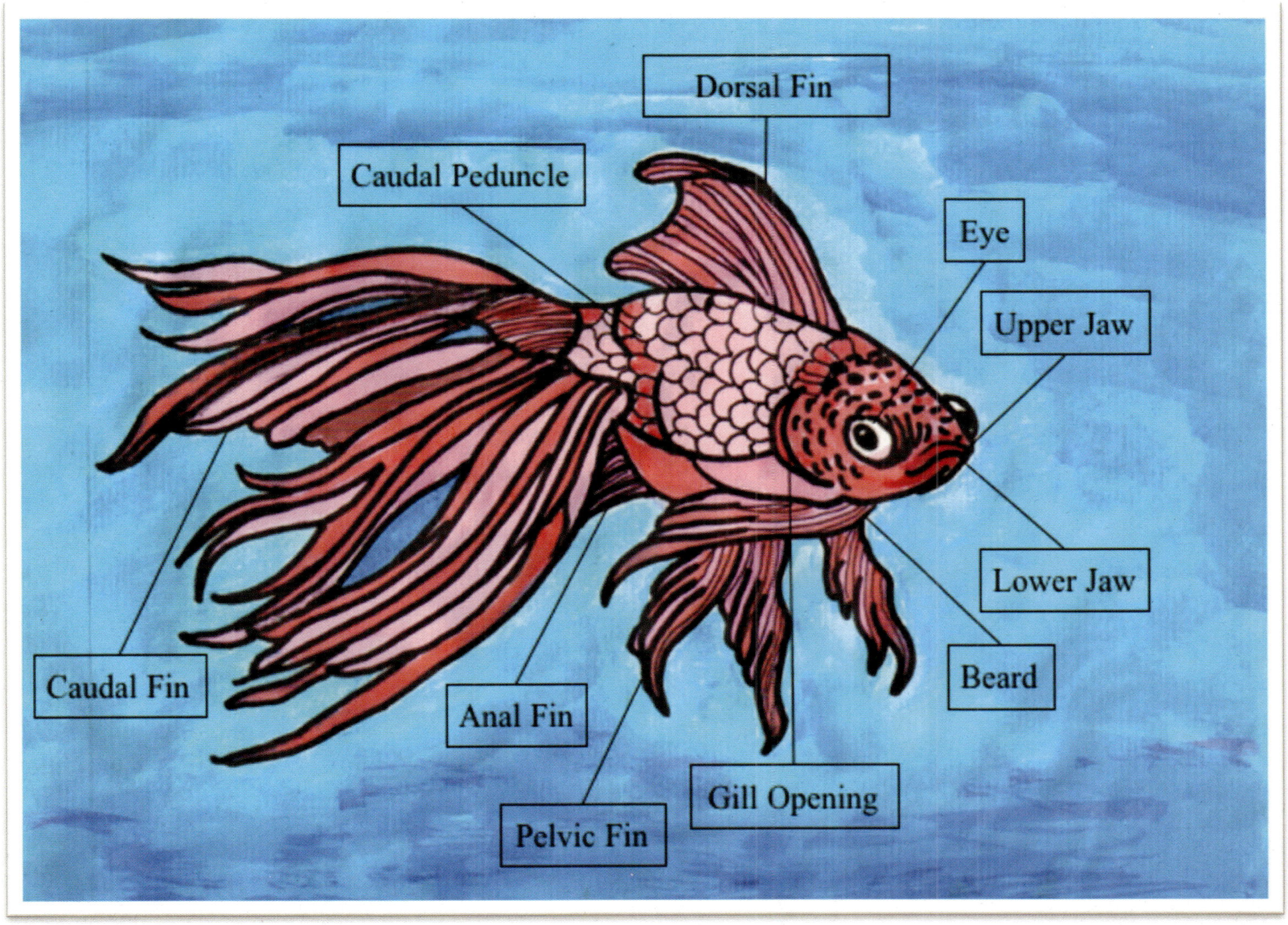

Anatomy of fish

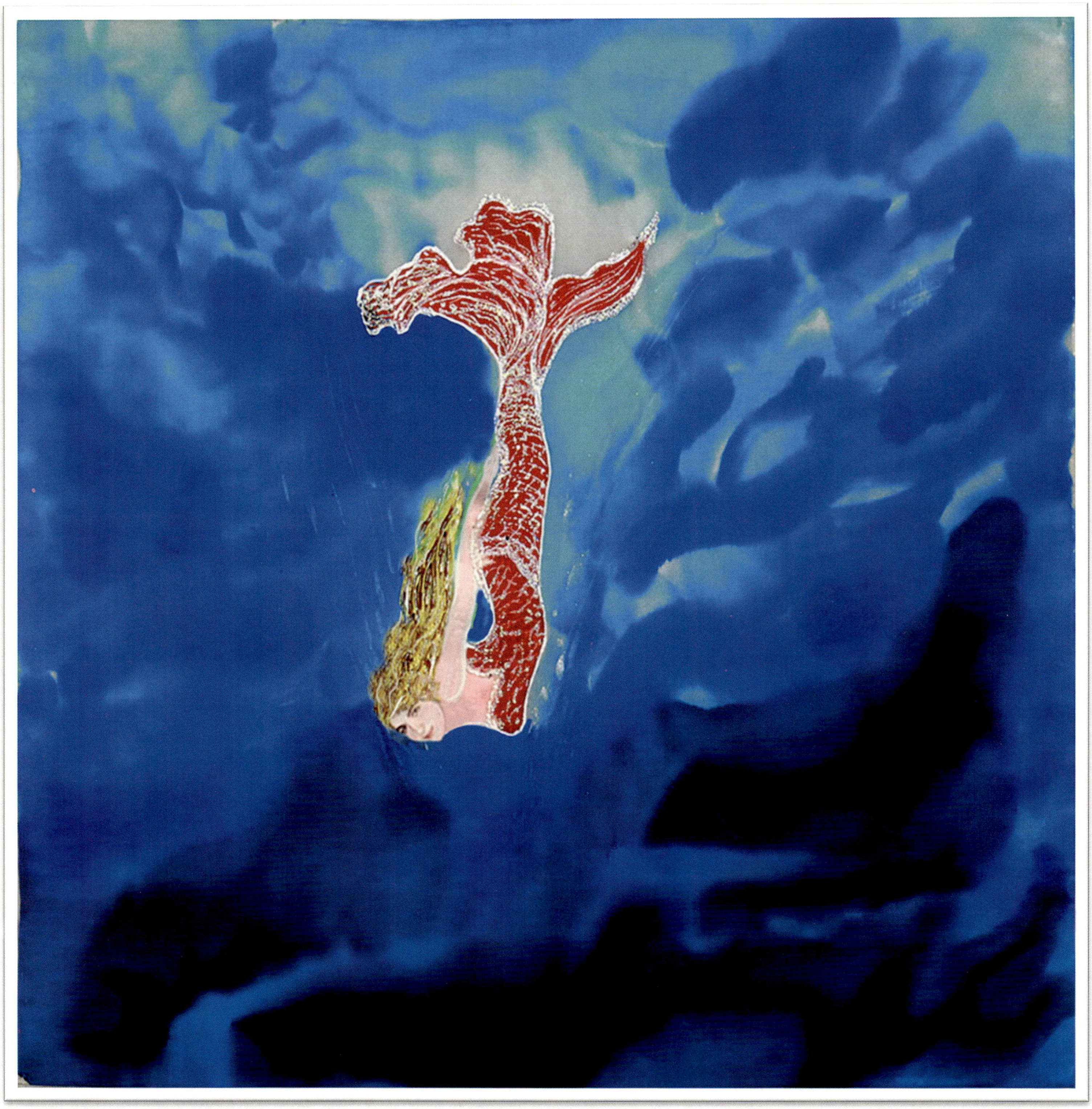

The peduncles looked like a mermaid's tail. Now Angel Liana looked like a real mermaid, and she was able to dive in easily, move around, and swim deeper into the water.

Since Angel Liana was used to having wings to fly and legs to walk to her destinations, swimming posed a big change and challenge for her. Now she had a mermaid tail and fish fins.

Soon she adapted herself to her environment and started enjoying her new situation. She felt excited that she was selected and trusted for the task.

Eager to start her big mission, she was ready to work hard in order to achieve it. She knew that every goal is accomplished only by wisdom and hard work.

She could already imagine what the finished work was going to look like. So she smiled, remained firm in her decision, and dived deeper in the water.

As she went further down, she saw different fish swimming and passing indifferently by her. Angel Liana realized that the seventh day was about to start, so she looked for a wide space with some large rocks.

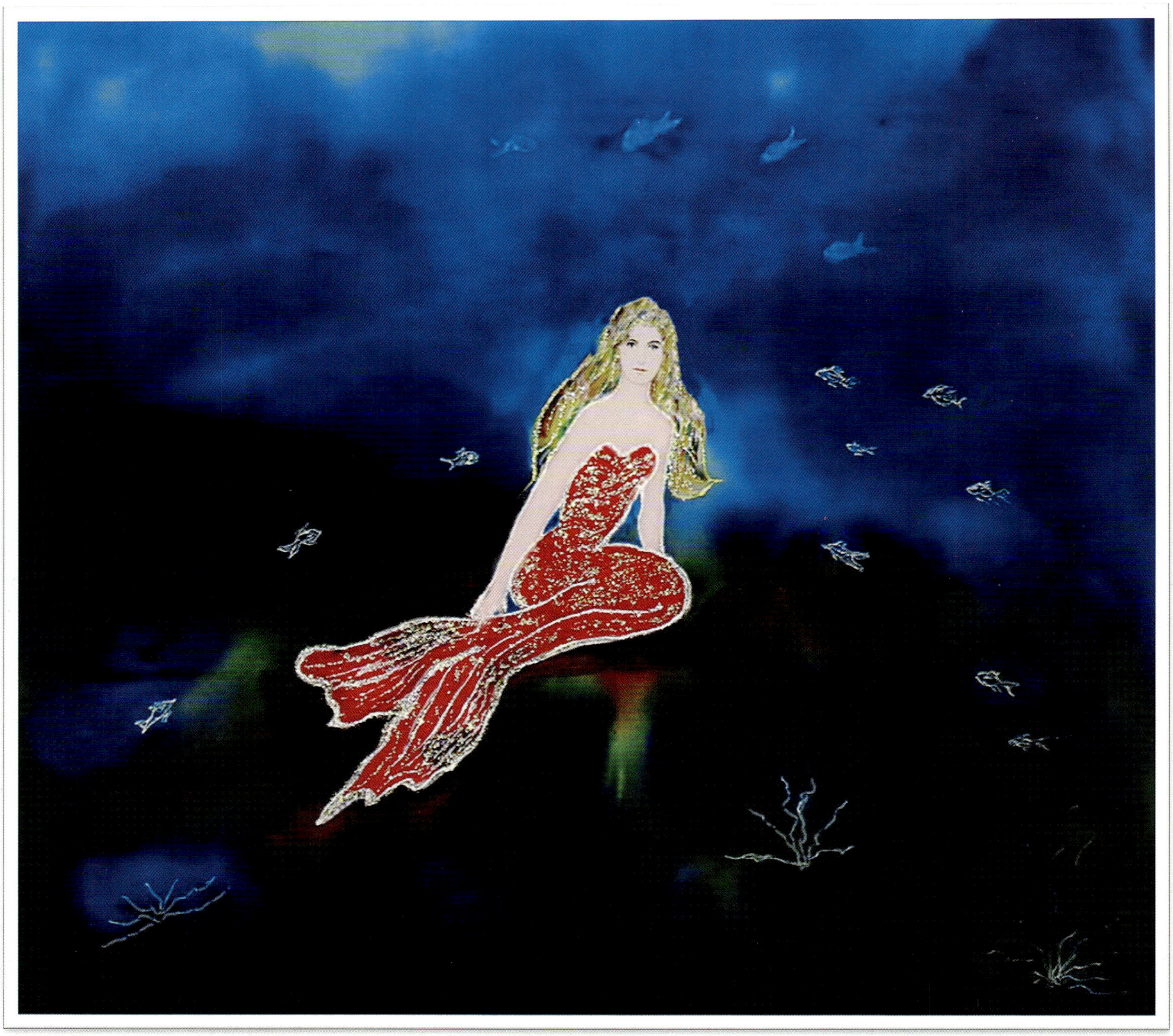

Very soon she found the proper place. As she settled and sat on one of the large stones, she noticed that beautiful underwater plants covered everything all around her. Different sizes of transparent fish were swimming curiously around this new creature.

Angel Liana rested on the seventh day while blessing and admiring all the existing beauty created deep in the water.

She started singing and praising God like she used to do every Shabbat with the angels in heaven. She felt sad since she missed her angel friends, but at that exact moment, a lot of different sizes of transparent fish surrounded her. They were all attracted by her sweet angelic voice. They circled her and stayed, quietly listening to her voice.

While all the fish were quietly resting around Angel Liana, one small, courageous, and curious fish asked her what kind of fish she was, since none of them had ever seen anything like her.

Angel Liana introduced herself and told them her name and explained her task. She said that since she was very knowledgeable in mixing colors, she was sent to them in order to make them look more beautiful. But, of course, this was only if they desired it. They had their free will and choice to stay as they were or change to a new look and colors.

She explained her plans to them and said that after Shabbat was over, she would start using her first primary color, which is yellow. For the entire first week, the fish that wanted to turn into yellow color could come to her and she will teach them how to do it.

She told them that they could turn into complete yellow color or save some parts of their bodies. That way, if they desired, they would be able to change to a different shade or add additional colors.

Some fish were very excited and said that they would be back the next day, early in the morning. Then everyone rested or slept.

Book Two
Yellow

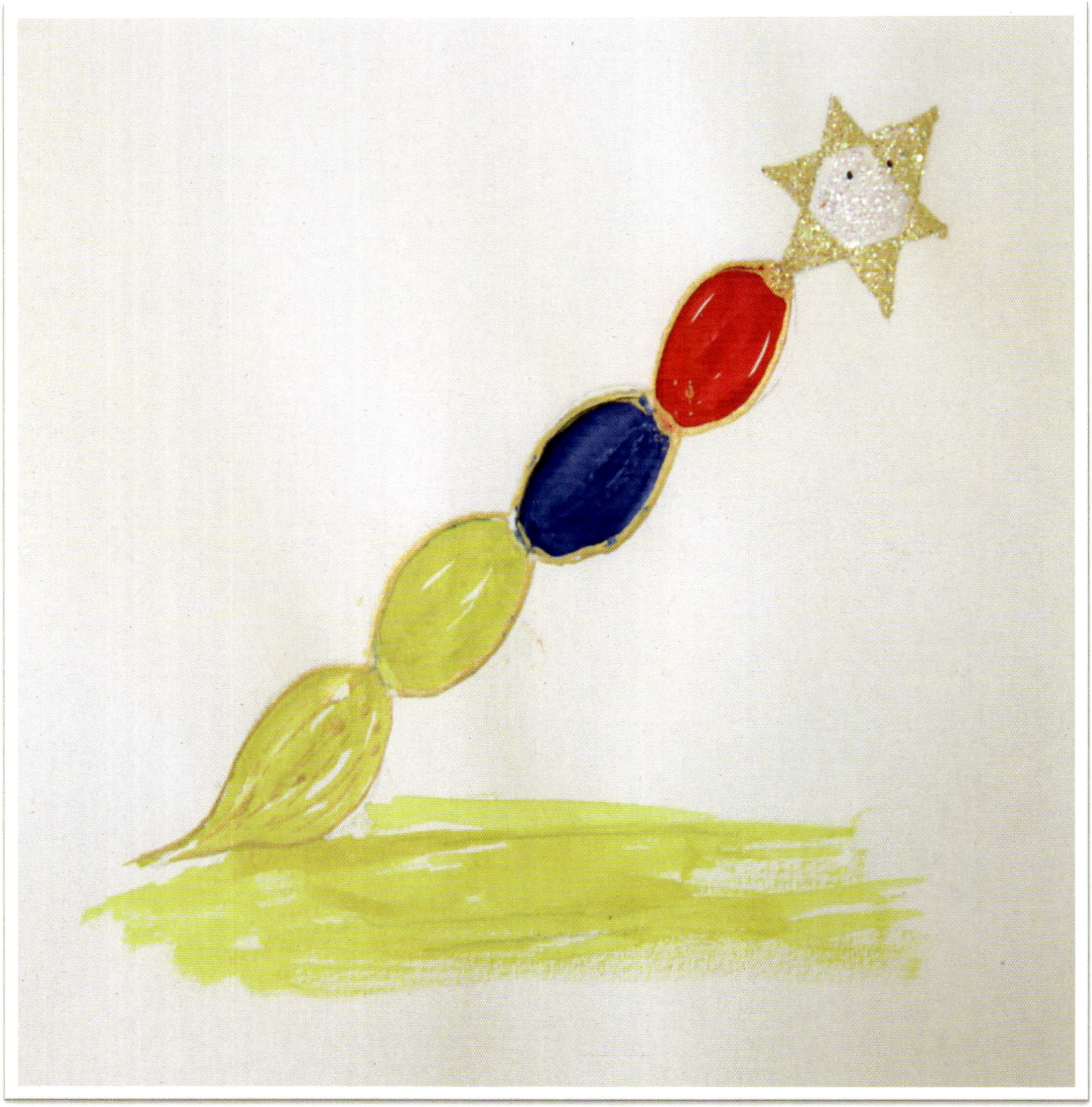

In the morning, Angel Liana chose some small shells. She hit them three times with the golden star of her magic brush, and the small shells turned into large containers.

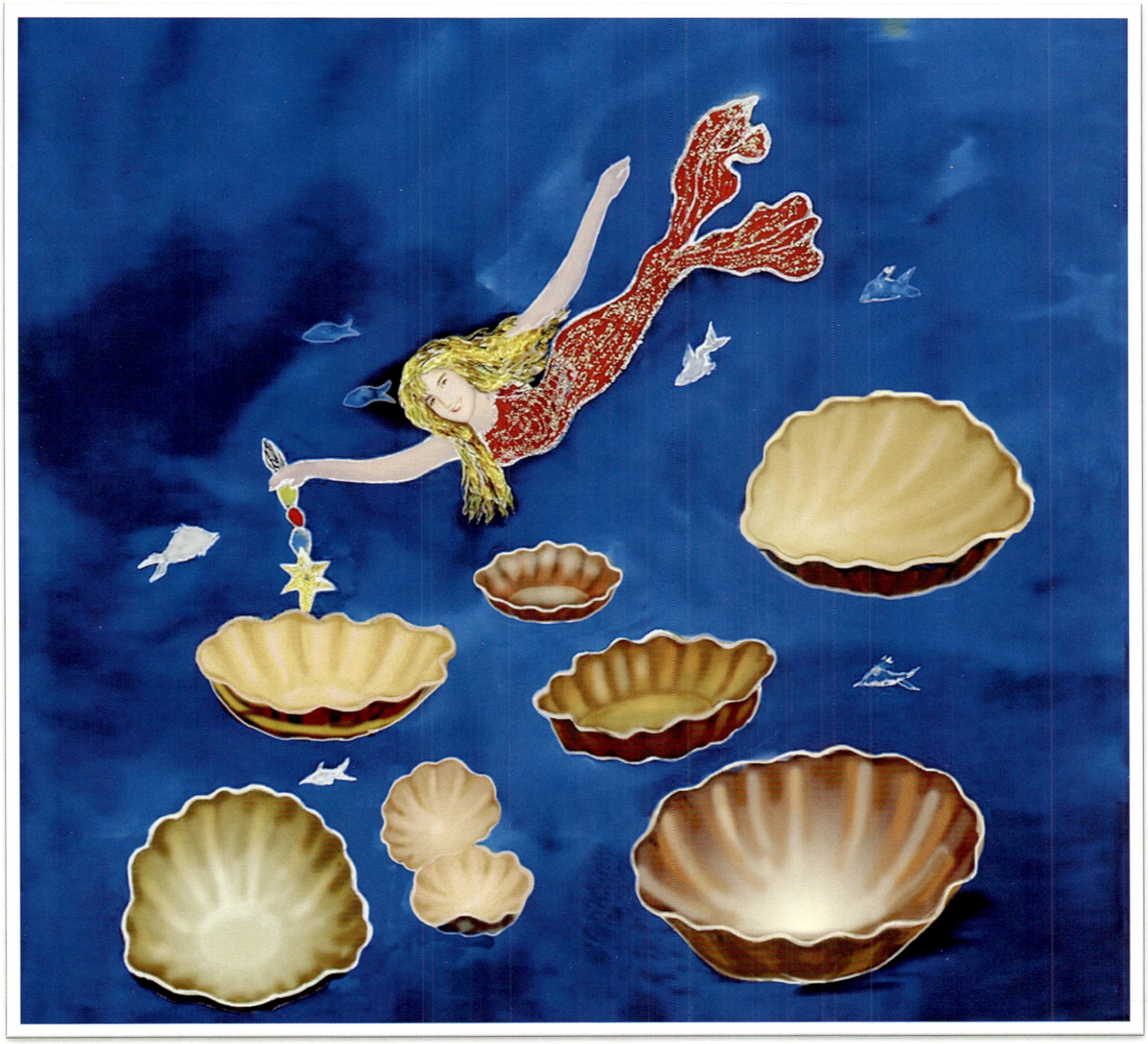

Then she unscrewed the yellow container, poured one drop of the concentrated yellow color into the shells, and filled the rest with water.

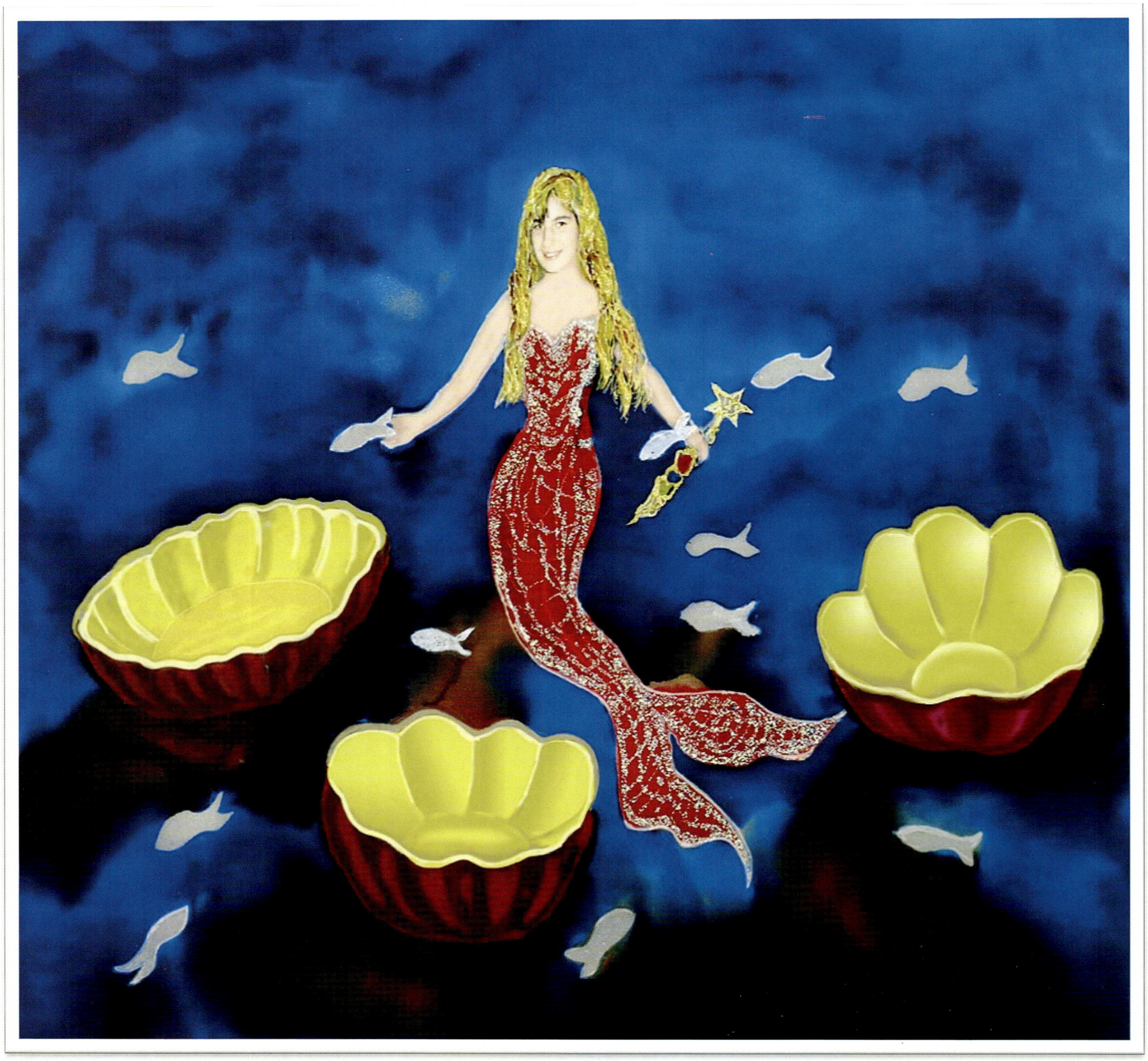

Different sizes and forms of fish were already in line, waiting anxiously to see how they could turn into yellow color.

When everything was ready, with the tip of the hair of the brush, she touched the yellow color in the shell, and made a small dot on the fish that was standing in front of the line. Then she asked all the other fish to look and see what happened.

All the fish waiting in the line were excited to see such a beautiful bright yellow color on the first fish. Another fish said that it reminded him of the color he had seen around the sun while swimming on the surface of the water one day!

So Angel Liana told them that if they wanted to become completely yellow, they would have to close their eyes and mouth, jump in the big mixing cups one by one, and then swim out.

The first fish closed his eyes and mouth, jumped in and then out, and said:
"Voila, I am the first beautiful yellow fish!"

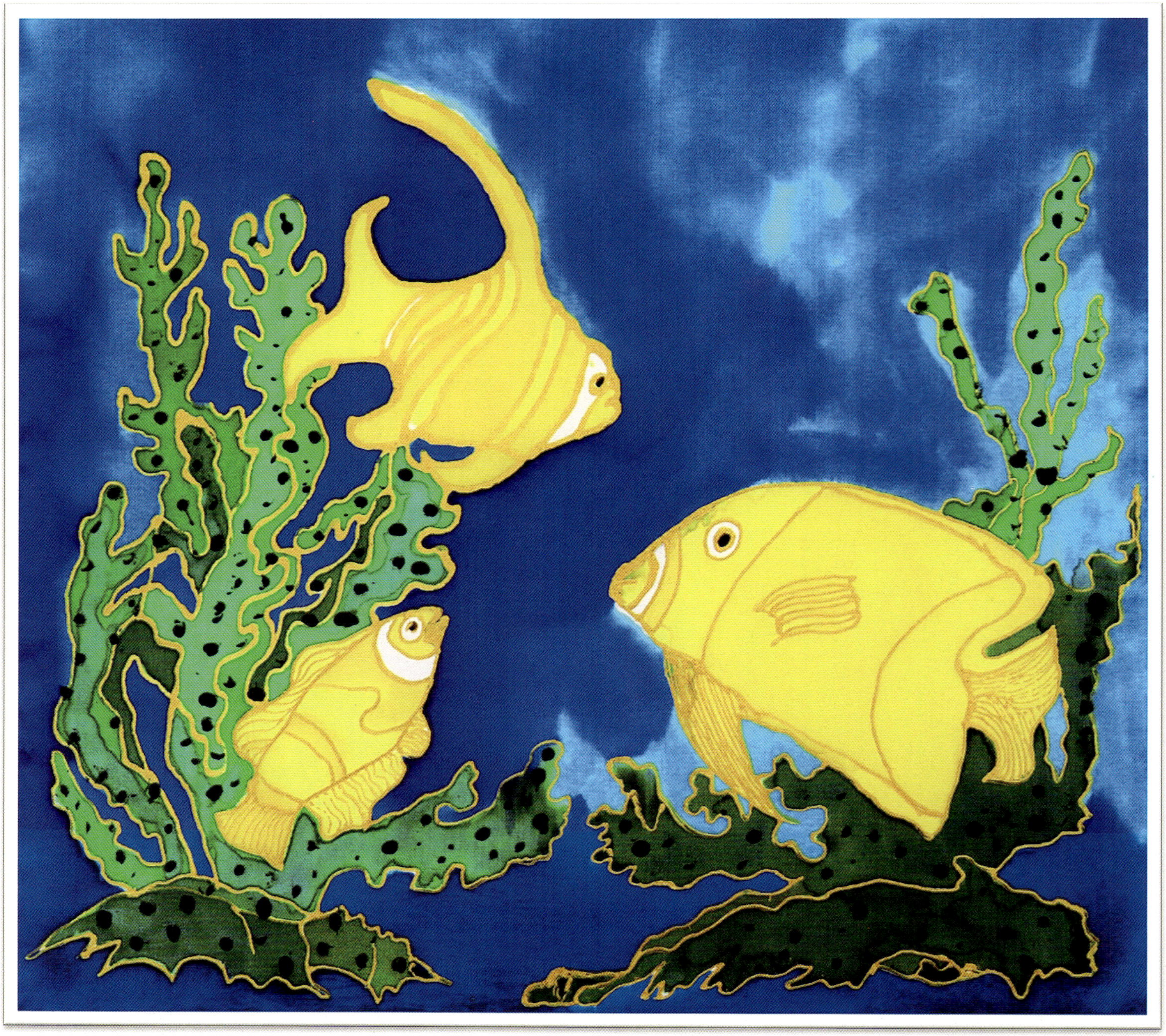

For the entire day, many small and large fish jumped in and out of the large mixing cups. By the end of the day, there were plenty of beautiful yellow fish swimming in the water, glowing and showing off their beautiful yellow color to all the other fish.

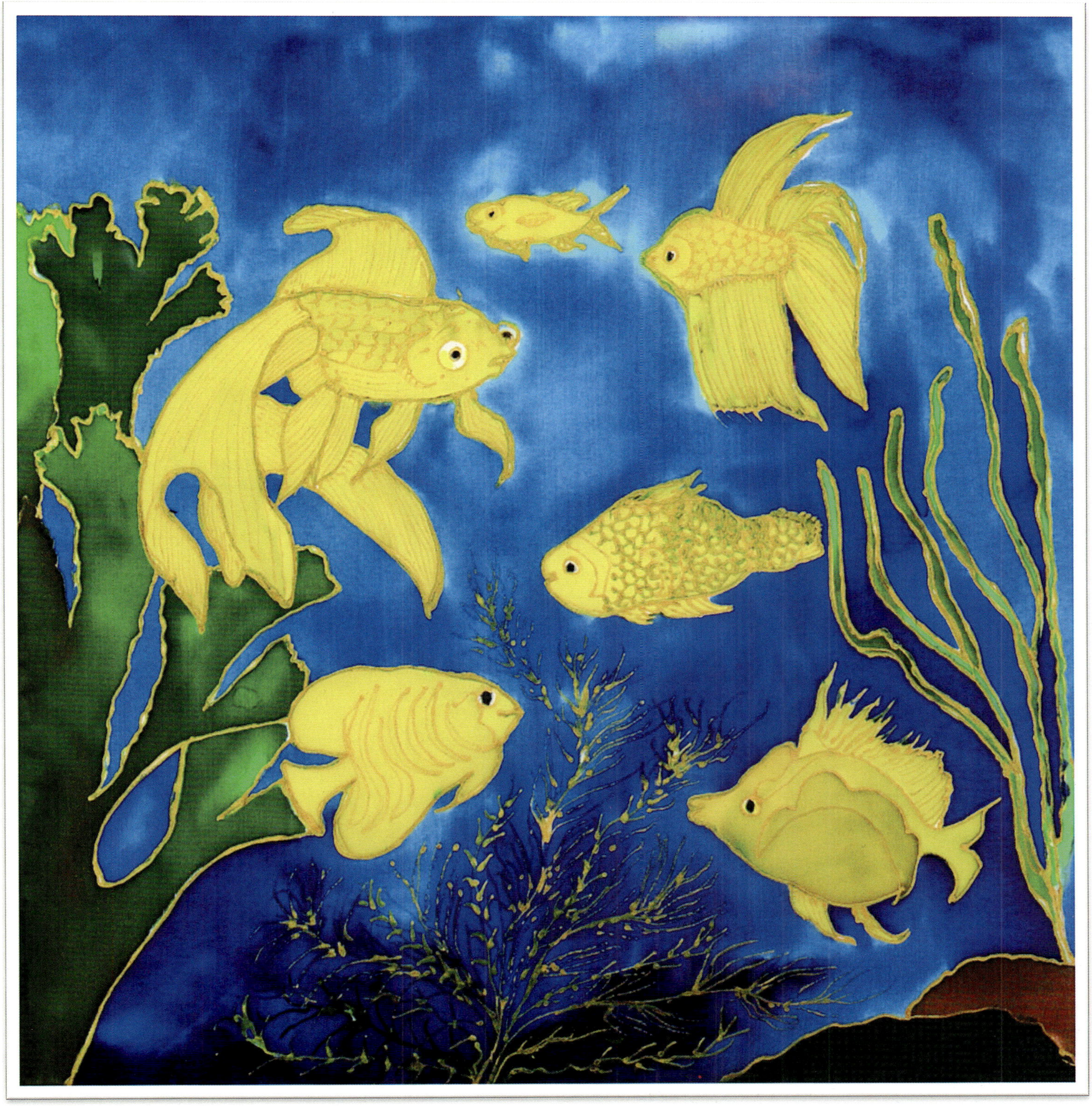

The next morning, when Angel Liana was ready for work, the line was already formed with excited fish of all sizes and forms. She told them:
"If you want to be yellow all over, just jump in the mixing cups, but remember to close your eyes and mouth while in the color. But, if you would like to have a design like strips and dots or other shapes, then do as I demonstrate."

She asked for a volunteer. The first fish standing on line approached. She wrapped the fish with a long seaweed strip by leaving some space in between, and then she secured the ends and asked the fish to enter in the mixing cup. After the fish came out of the color, she pulled out the seaweed strip and—surprise! — the fish had yellow and transparent stripes all over.

All the fish in line were excited and wanted to imitate these stripes immediately. But Angel Liana told them: "Let me show you all the possibilities that you have and then you choose the one that you like best."

She asked for another volunteer and a large fish approached. Angel Liana gently pushed some of the empty shells on the fish and asked him to enter the container. When the fish came out, it had clear and yellow dots and shapes on its body. The shells were also decorated in yellow color. More excited fish wanted to have the dots on their bodies.

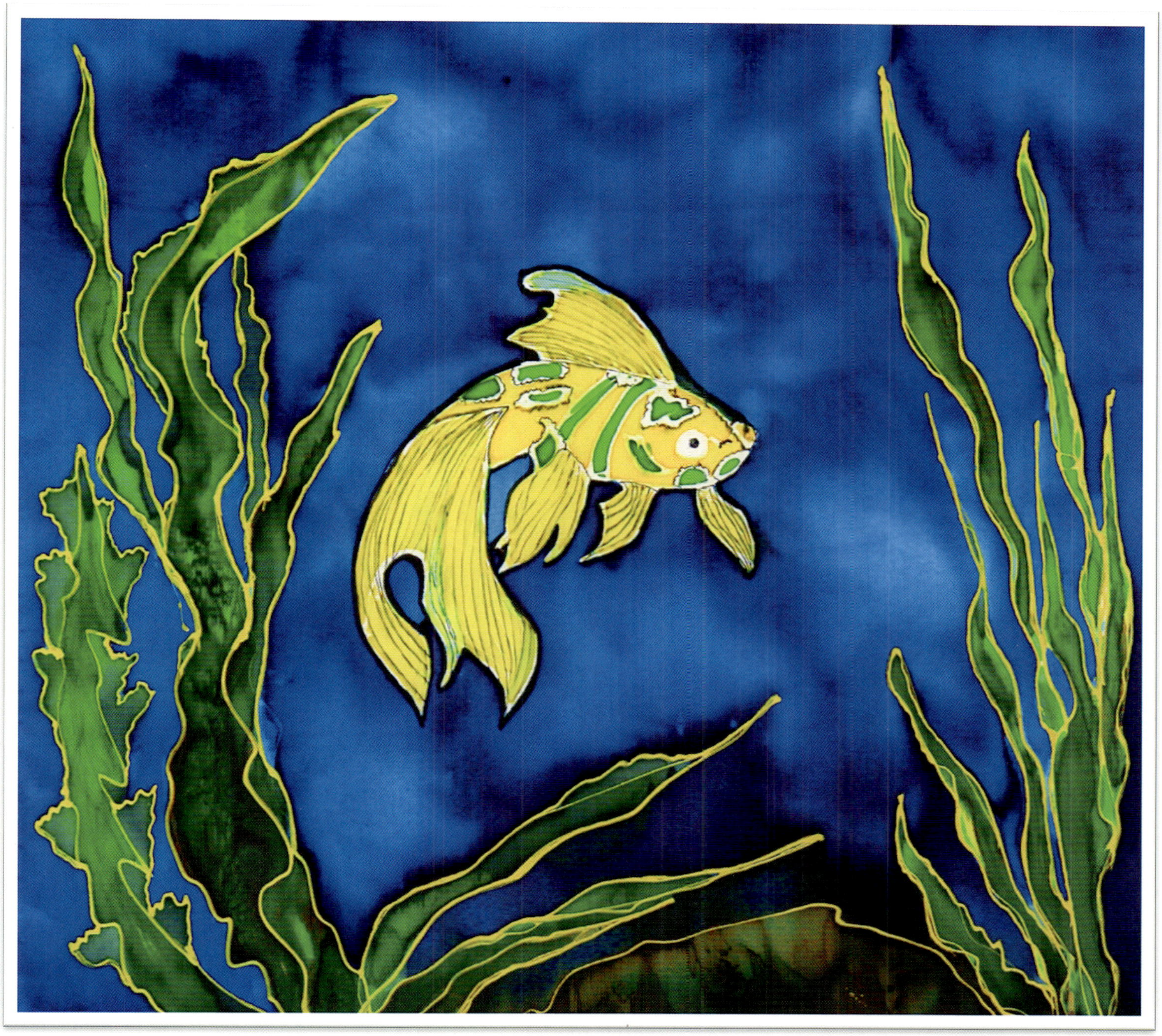

Angel Liana had already prepared some seaweed in different shapes: squares, triangles, stars, and many others. So she demonstrated other techniques of sticking the various shapes and many other designs on their bodies.

Some fish made big bubbles with their mouths and sent them to the surface of the water, like celebrating balloons, and thanked her. They said that she was amazing to do all this magic with one color. But Angel Liana's face turned sad. She told them gently that they should never make a mistake in using this word.

She said: "What I perform is not called magic; nor a miracle. I have studied and practiced for a long time to obtain the knowledge of mixing colors. With passing time and experience, I have become a real colorist. God is the only one who is able to create miracles. If you ask your parents and grandparents, they will be able to tell you amazing stories, since they have experienced and seen many of God's 'miracles.' If you learn all that I am teaching you today and work hard, in time you will become like me and will be able to teach the art of coloring to your children and others in the future."

For the rest of the week, many fish decorated their bodies in solid yellow, yellow stripes, yellow dots, yellow squares, and other shapes with yellow.

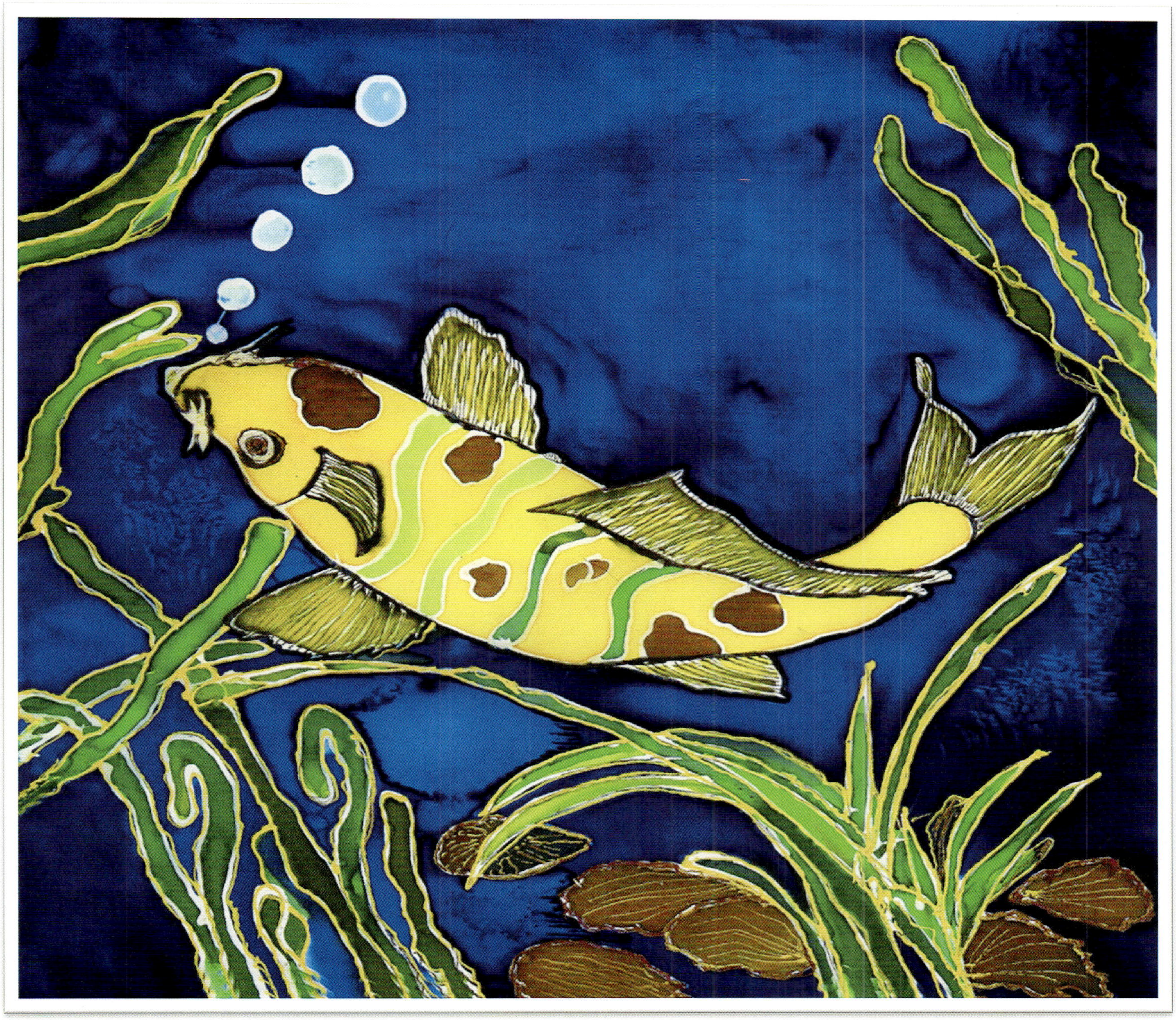

The water was full of beautiful, happy, and bright yellow colors. Some underwater plants, creatures, and shells also wanted to turn to yellow and asked permission and were allowed to change. Some of the stones and rocks around them had also received splashes of yellow colors in different intensity of shades and shapes.

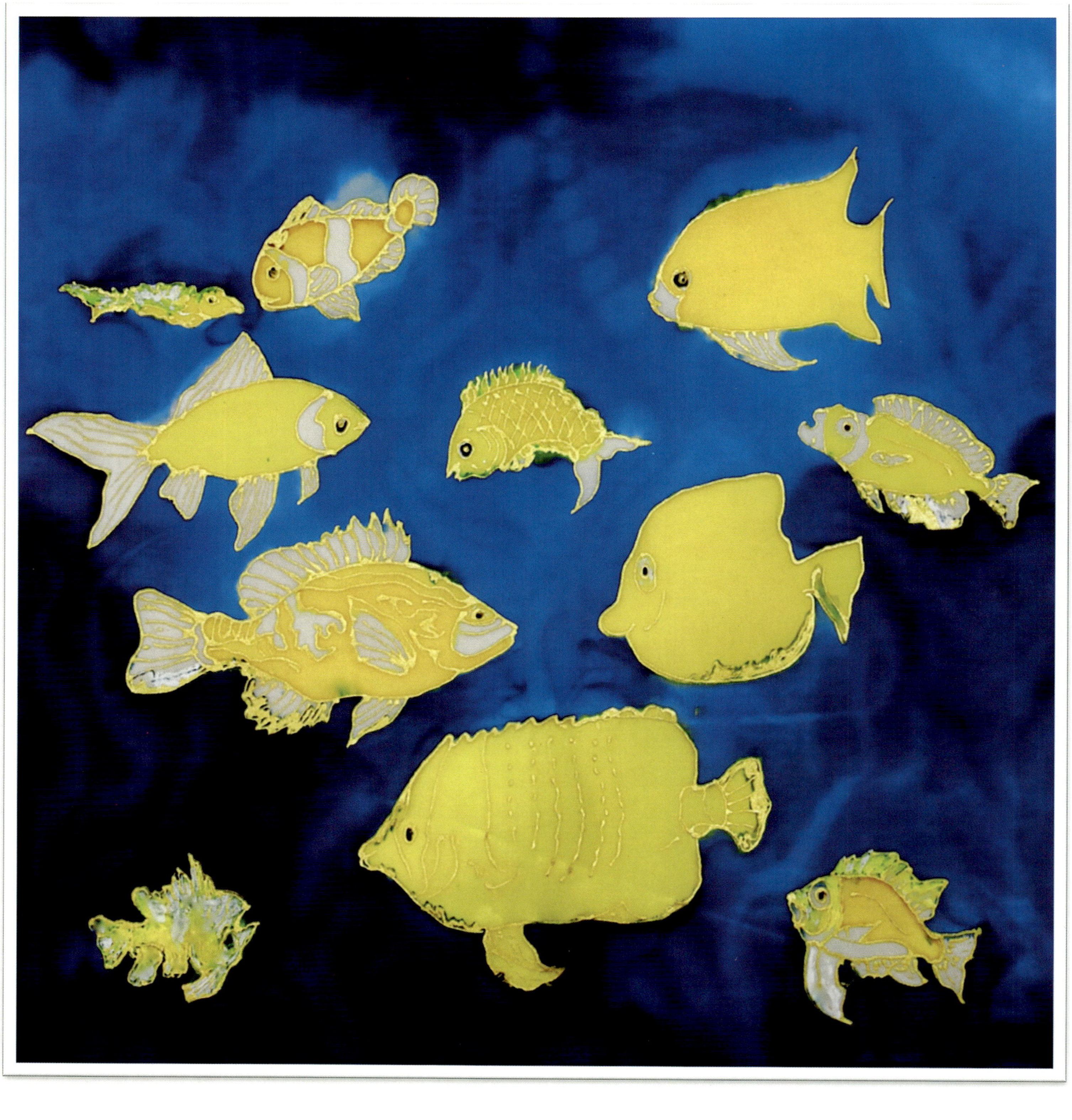

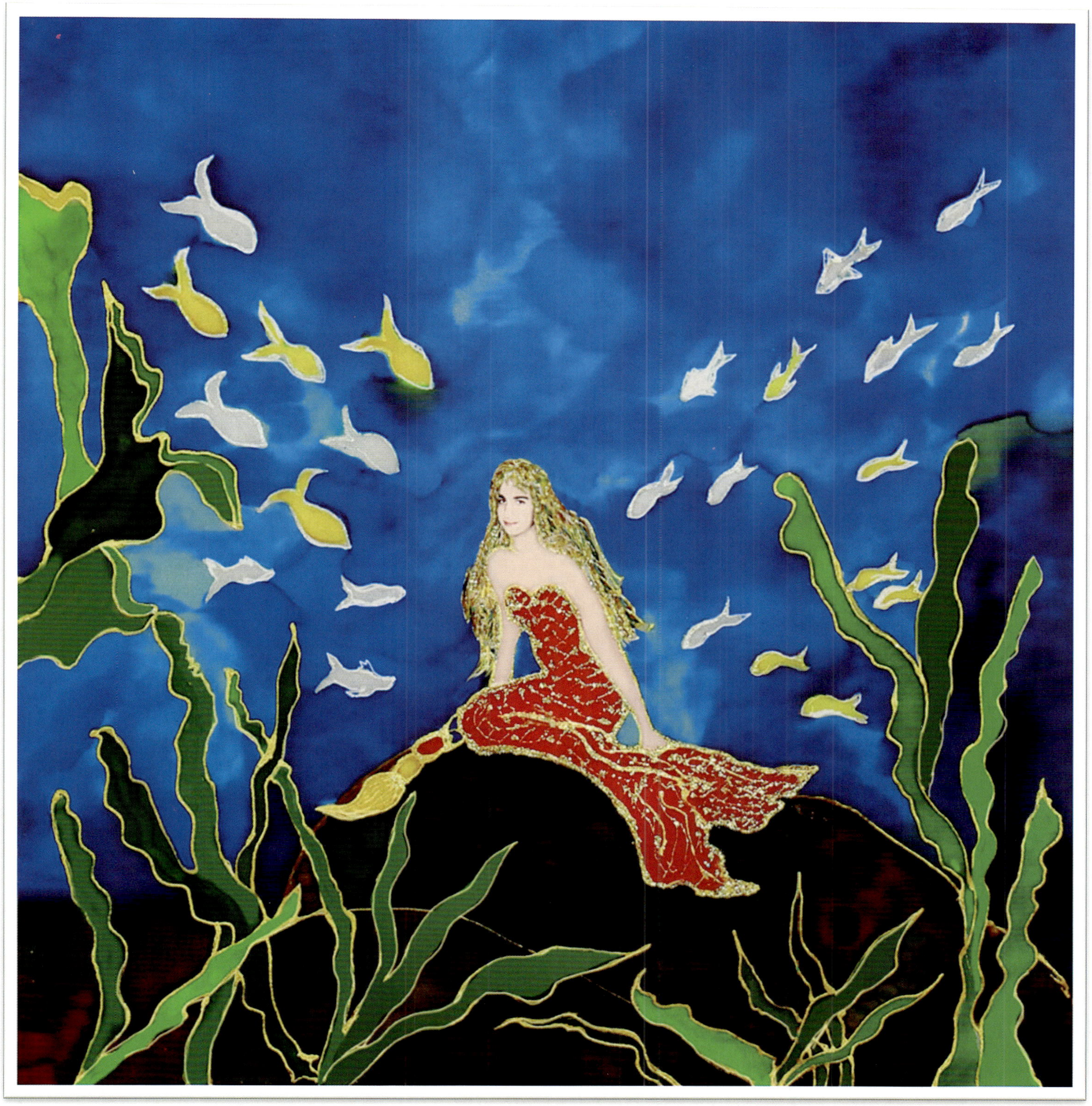

And God was watching his angel from the heavens and was satisfied with the result of her hard work.

On the evening of the sixth day, Angel Liana told the fish that the next day was the seventh day, so they would all rest and admire the beauty of the yellow color that they had created in a week.

A very beautiful small yellow fish asked her: “Can we come and surround you like we did last week? Would you tell us stories and sing for us? I love your angelic voice.”

Angel Liana smiled and replied of course—come! I will tell you some of the creation stories and will sing for you. Now we all have to rest and thank God for our friendship, this opportunity, and the work that we have accomplished together all this week. Next week we are going to learn about another new exciting color: Red.

Book Three
Red

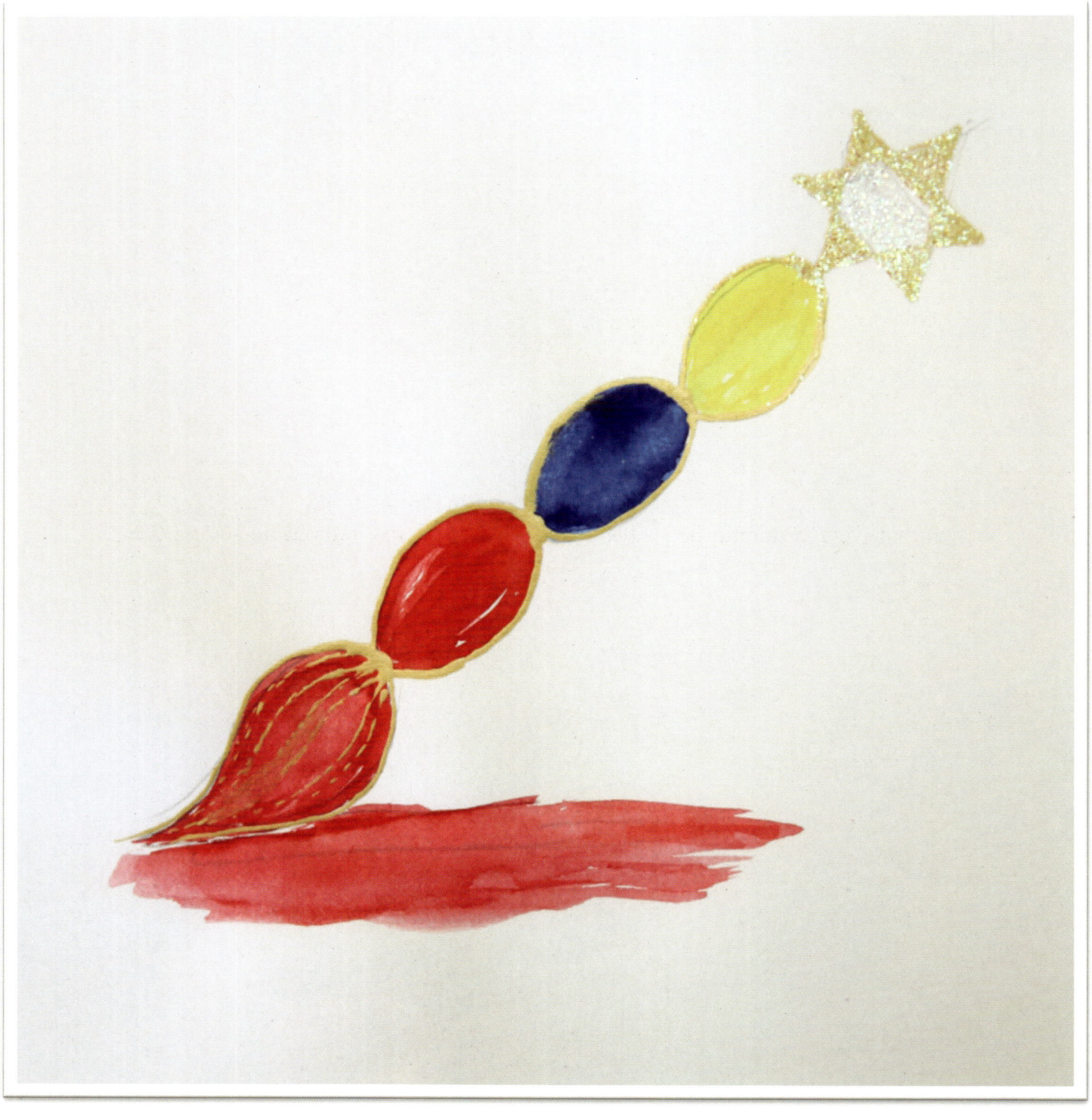

The next morning Angel Liana woke up very early. It was the second week that she had left the heavens and her friends. Now she was getting ready to start the second week of her work underwater, coloring the fish.

She found some new empty shells. She gently struck them three times with the golden star of the brush, and the little shells turned into large mixing cups and containers.

Angel Liana opened the second section of her brush; she dropped a small dot of red color into the mixing cup and filled it with water. All the surrounding fish that were watching her work cried loudly with excitement on seeing the beautiful, bright Red color appear in the shell.

The line of fish was already formed. Now, most of the fish had learned and seen how some of them had changed to a solid or decorated yellow color.

The fish that had decided to become red were anxiously waiting in line to change their look. When all the preparatory work was accomplished, Angel Liana told them that it was time for the first fish on line to jump in the red color. Since they had already seen the different designs, they could choose to turn into solid red color or become decorated with stripes, dots and other forms.

The first fish jumped in the mixing cup and, as it swam out, on seeing the bright and beautiful red color, they all cried happily: “Red!”

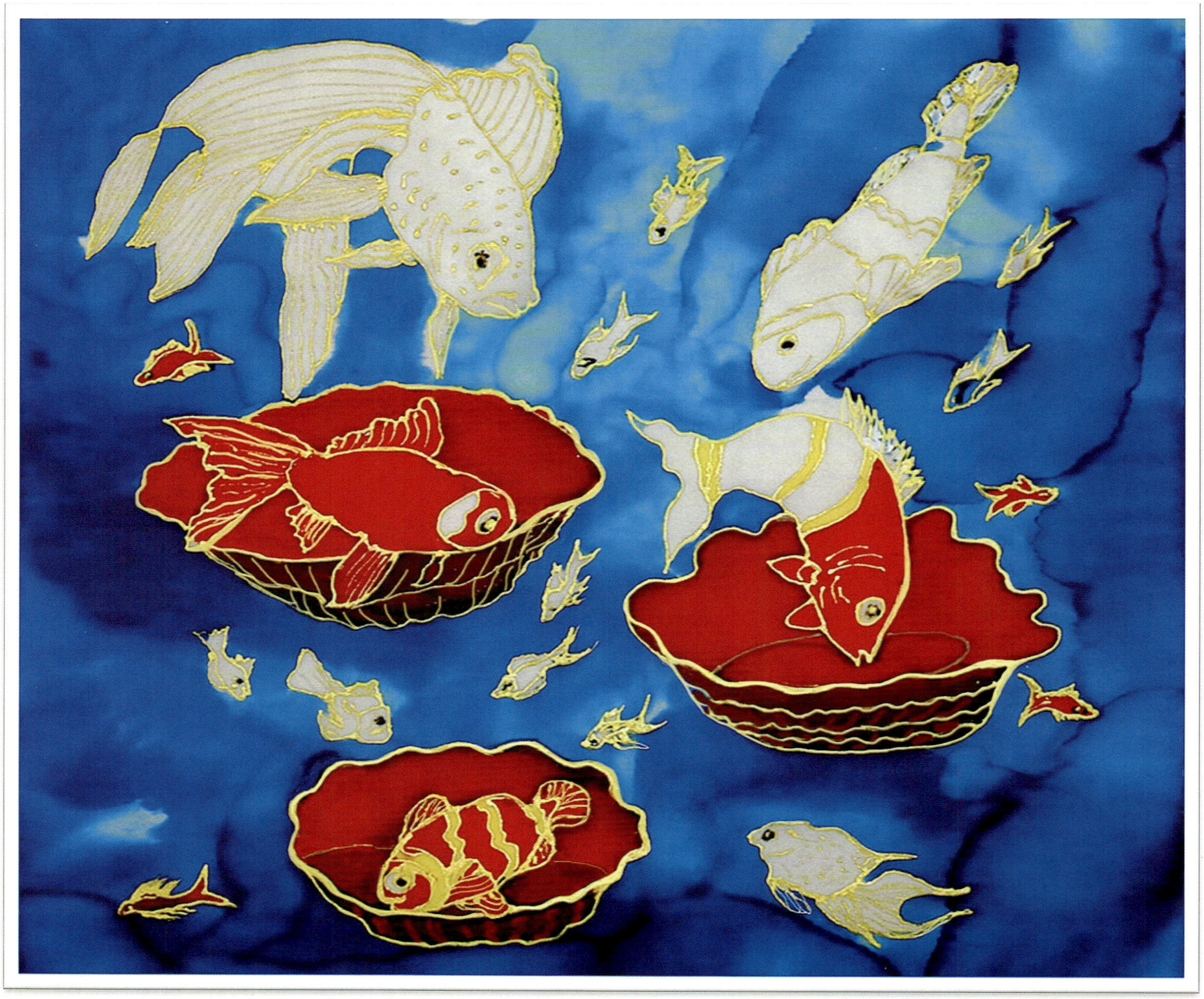

More fish jumped in and out, then the more creative ones started using seaweed strips and shells in order to preserve some of their transparent colors.

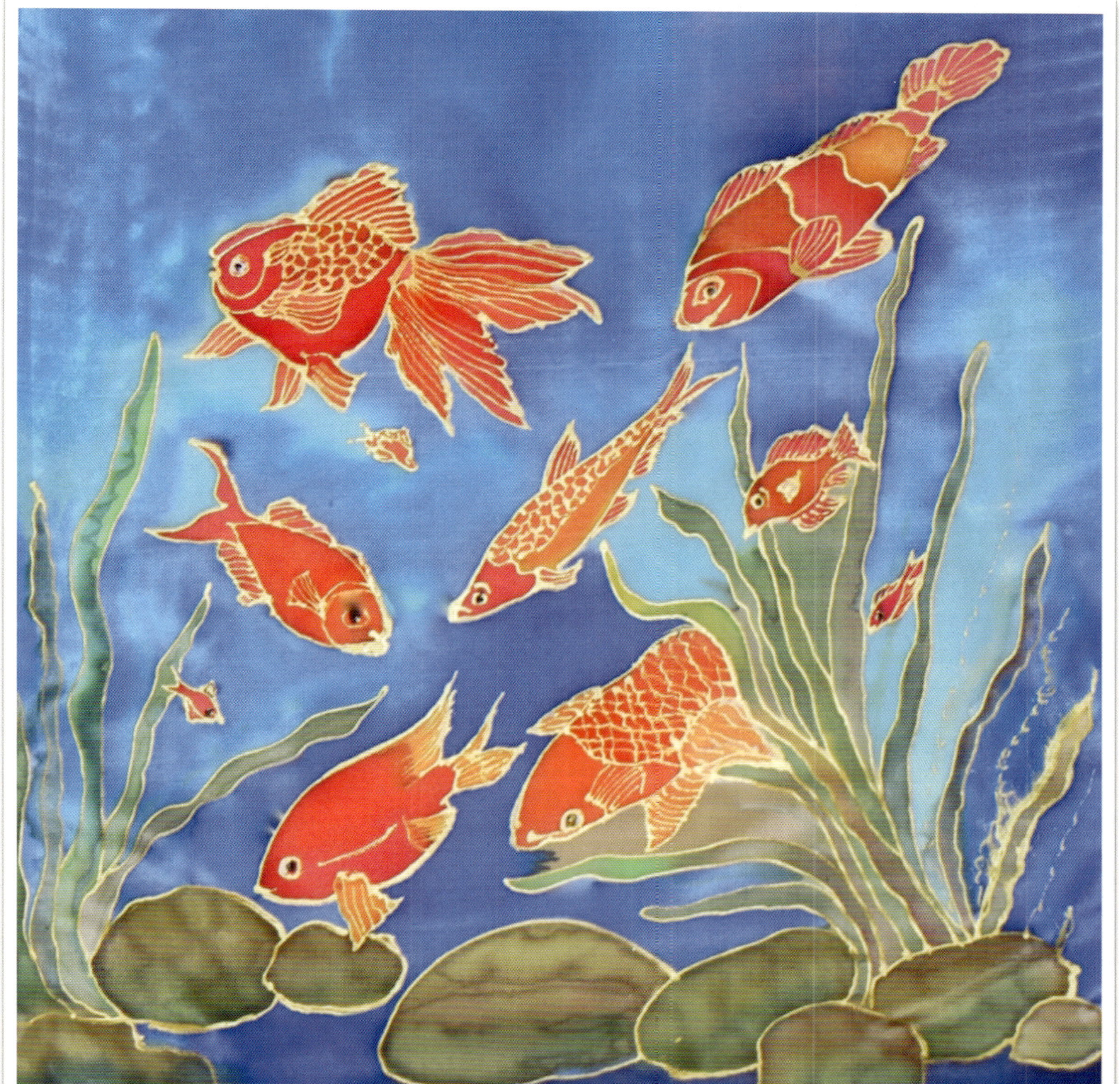

But then a question came up: some of the yellow fish asked Angel Liana if they could have some red colors too.

Angel Liana asked for a volunteer fish with yellow stripes that did not mind changing colors. She then covered all the yellow stripes with seaweed strips, but left one yellow strip out. Then she asked the fish to jump in the red dye.

Angel Liana took away the seaweed and explained: "As you can see, the parts that were covered with the seaweed kept their yellow color. But the parts that were not wrapped with the seaweed are now colored with red. And the one yellow strip, which I intentionally left unwrapped, turned into orange color."

YELLOW + RED = ORANGE
(The mixture result is from dark orange to the lightest color – gold)

RED + YELLOW = ORANGE
(The mixture results is from light orange to the darkest color – red)

Then Angel Liana said, “But there is a catch.” She explained that:

More yellow + less red = light orange

Less yellow + more red = dark orange

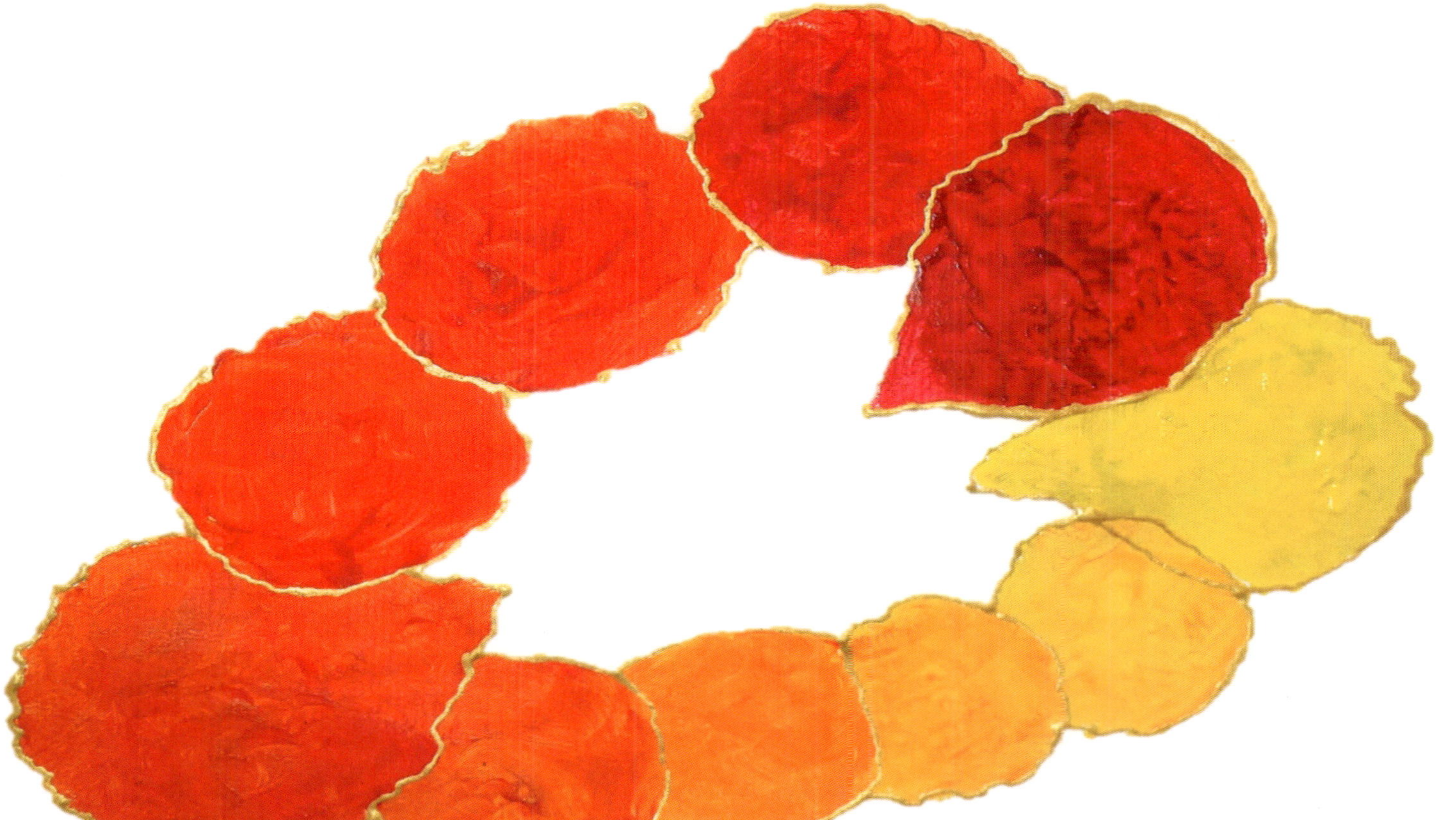

Different shades of orange created by mixing different drops of yellow and red.

This flower is painted by different shades of orange.

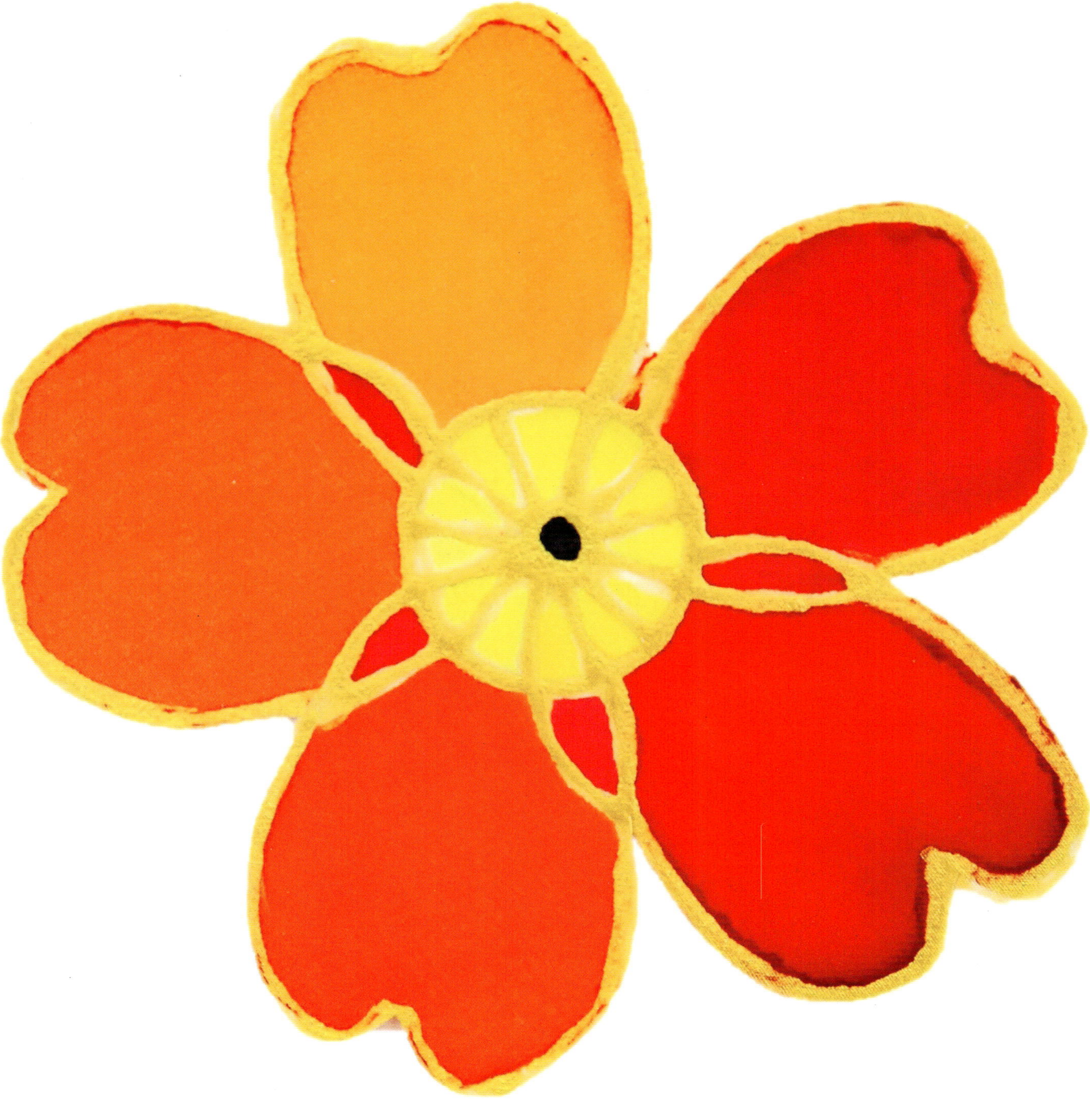

Angel Liana added:

“Now I have taught you the basic formula. A studious and curious fish will practice more, as I have done for many years. Mix the different amounts of yellow and red together and see what happens. Well, children, you too must take a notebook, like a real chemist in a laboratory. Write all your formulas down and put the given color next to your formula. I will give you a work sheet and you can multiply it when needed.”

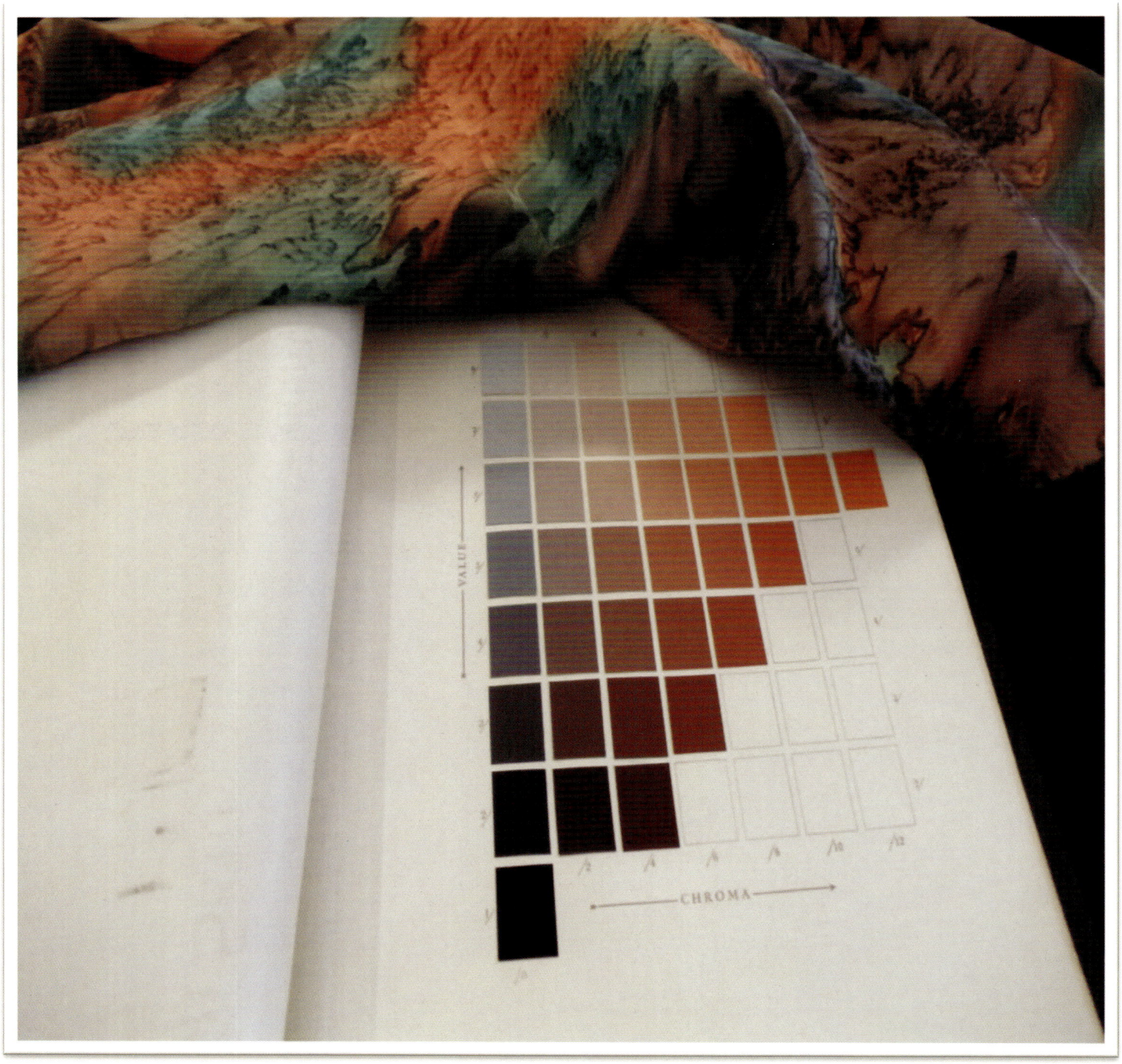

A professional way of registering the formulas.

Book Four
Blue

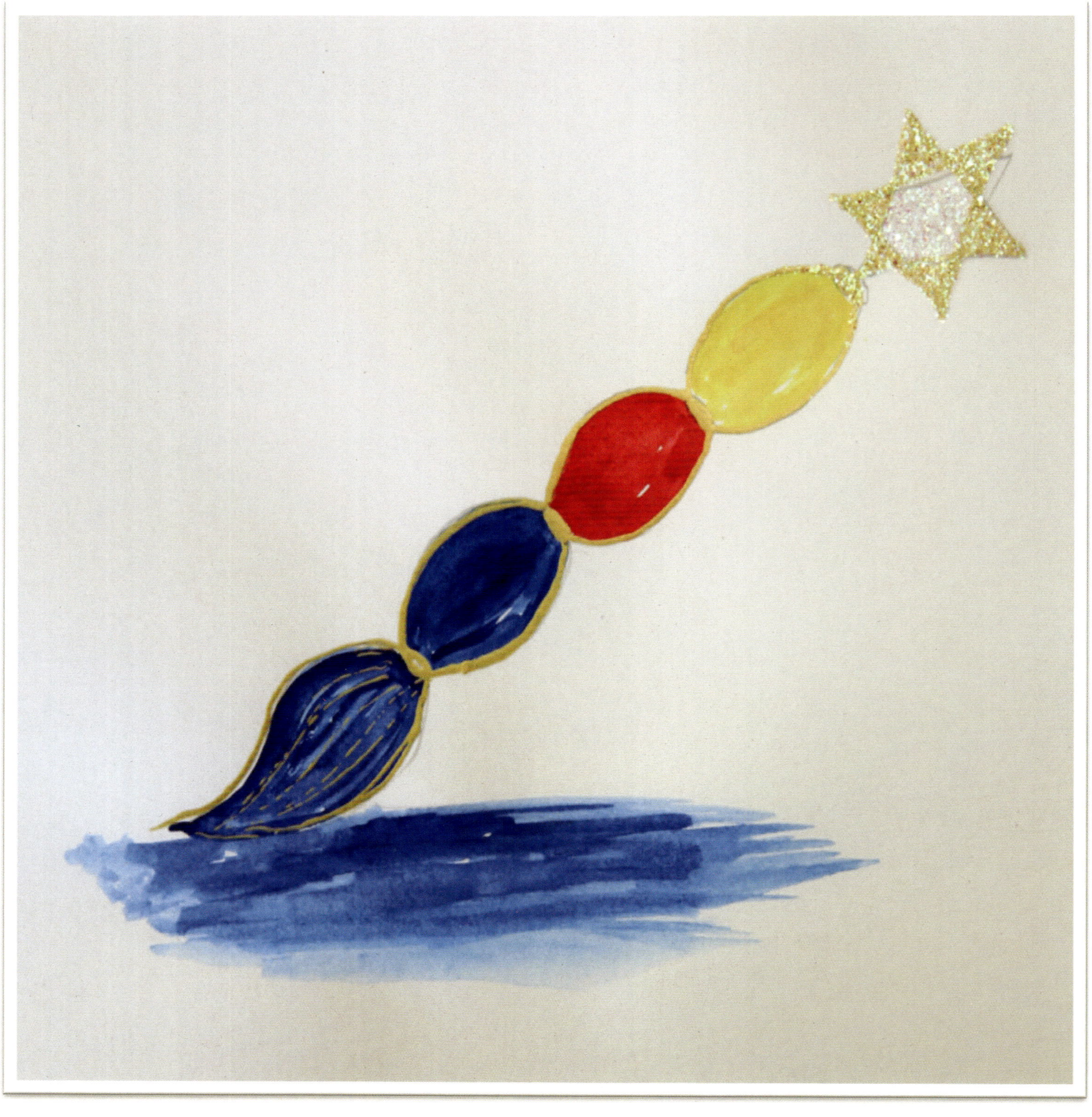

Angel Liana continued the same work with the blue colors. Since the fish had obtained some experience, it was easier to use the blue color, either solid or with different designs. But since some fish were already colored in red and yellow, they started turning into different shades of green and purple.

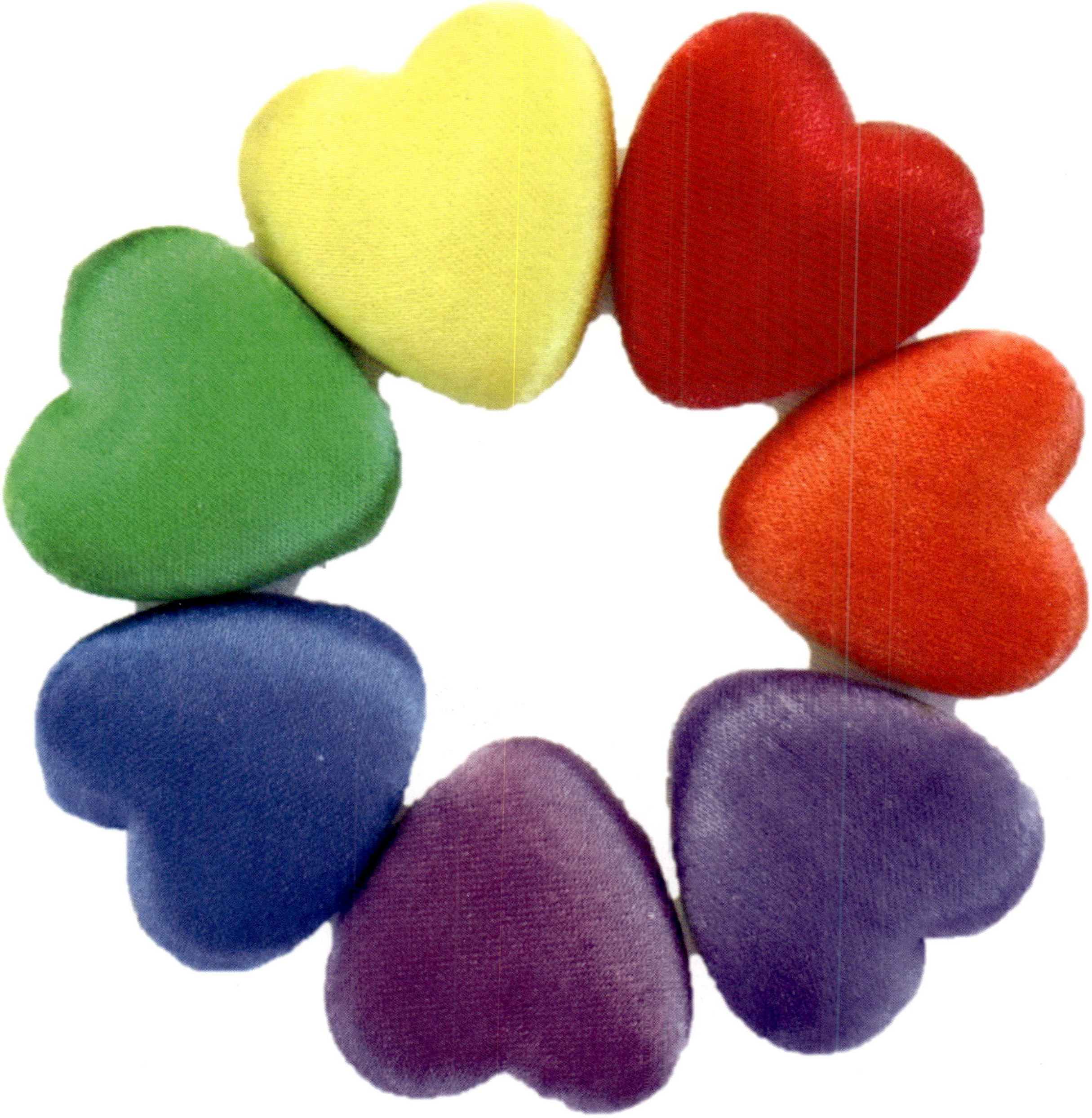

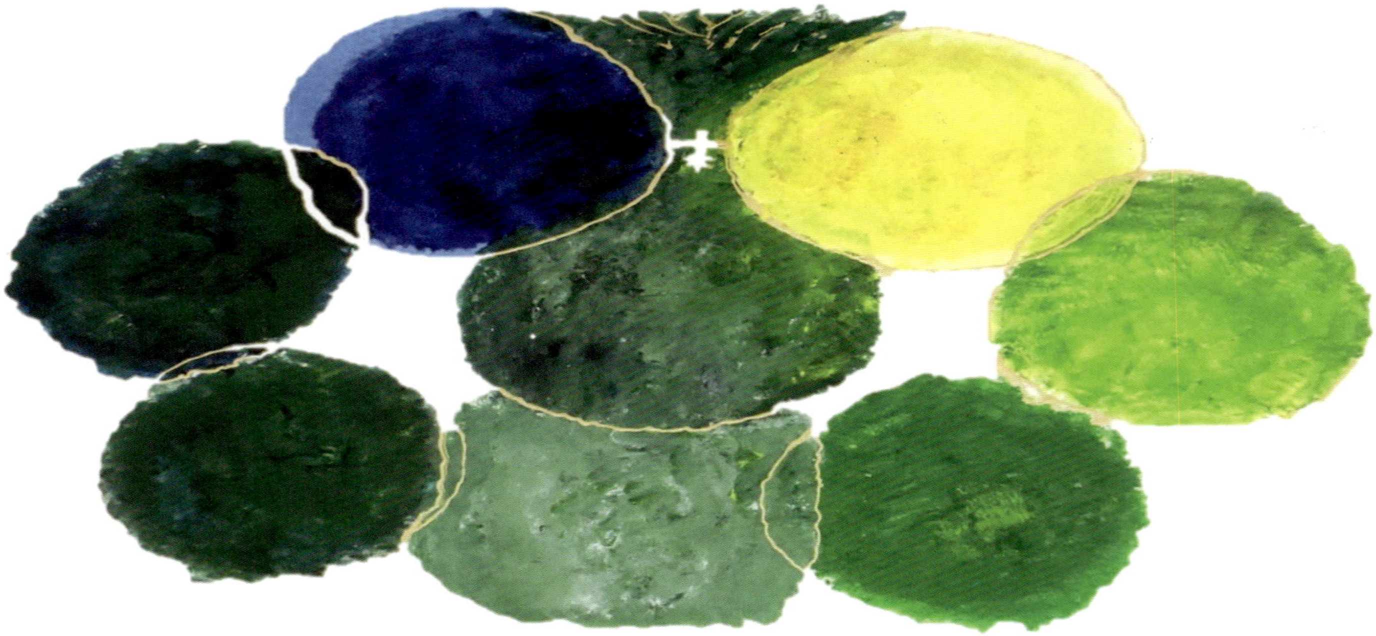

blue + yellow = green

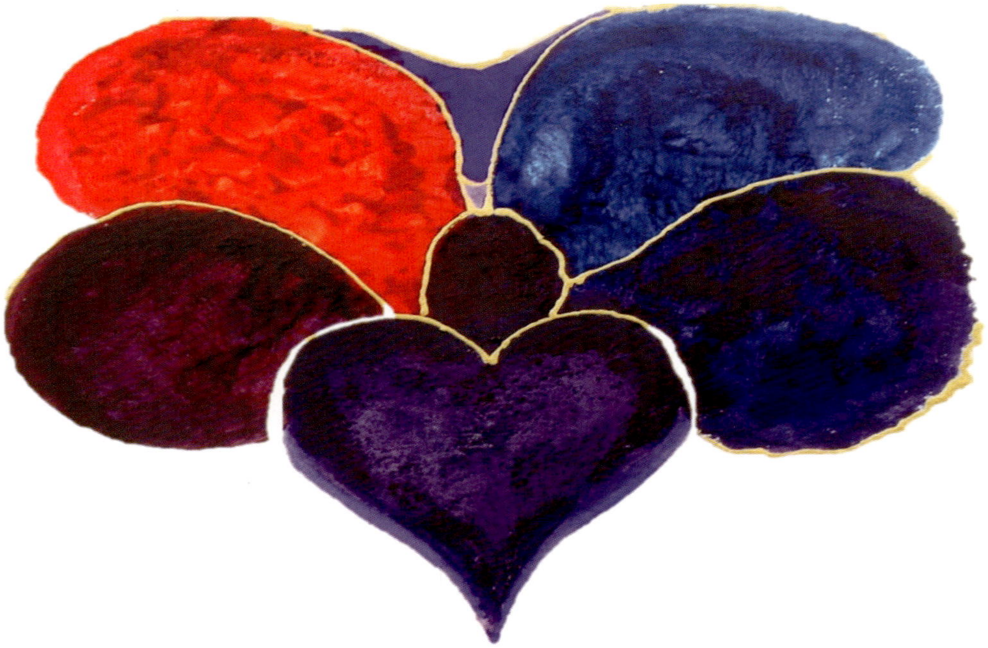

blue + red = violet

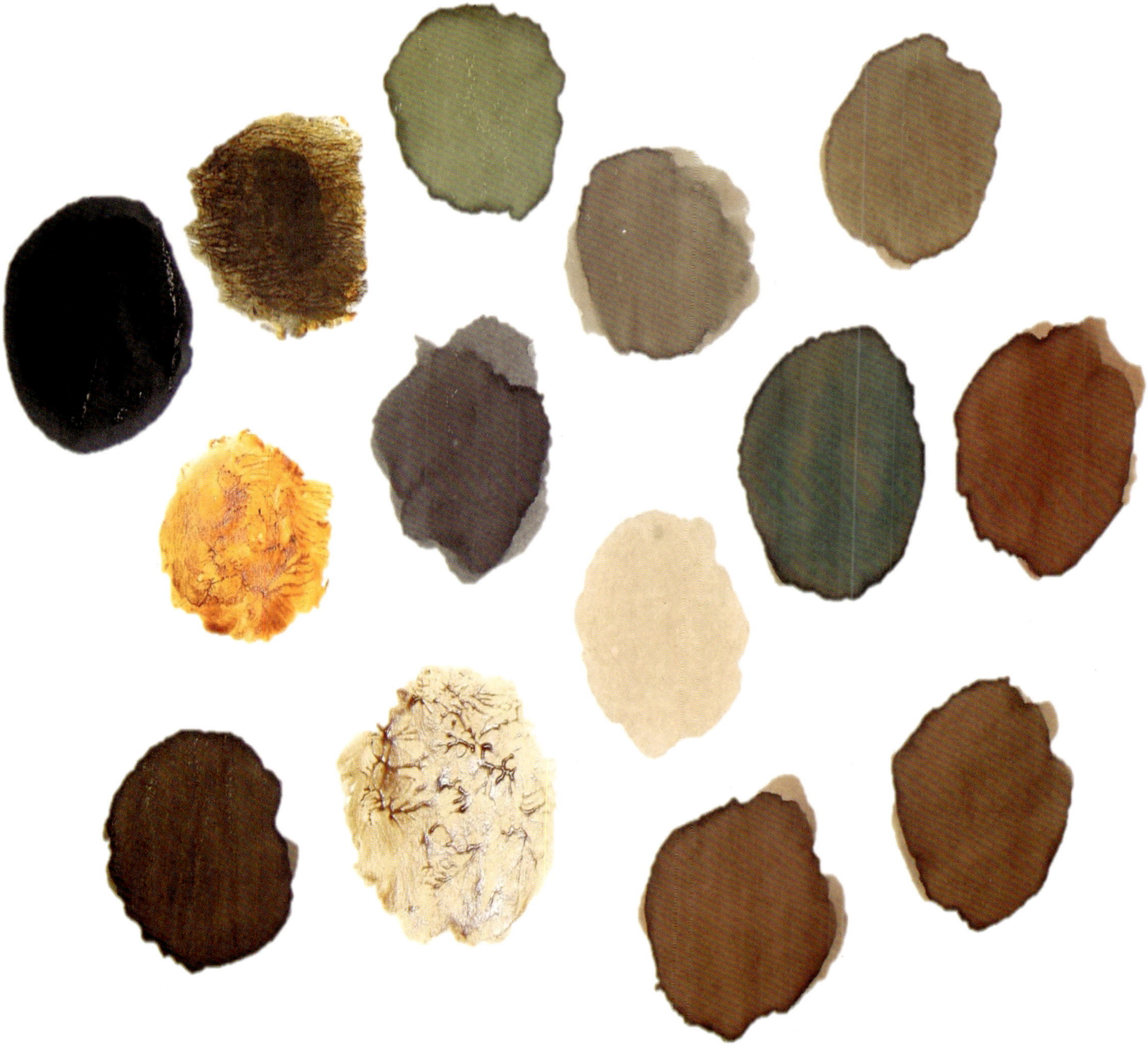

Different shades of browns

Find the formulas for the different shades of browns and share them with Angel Liana

Surprise—some fish turned into brown and black colors! Can you find the formula? You already know how to obtain brown and black colors by mixing three colors together. But now you can find formulas for different shades of browns and blacks—for example dark brown, reddish brown, gold brown, and the same for black, navy, and night black.

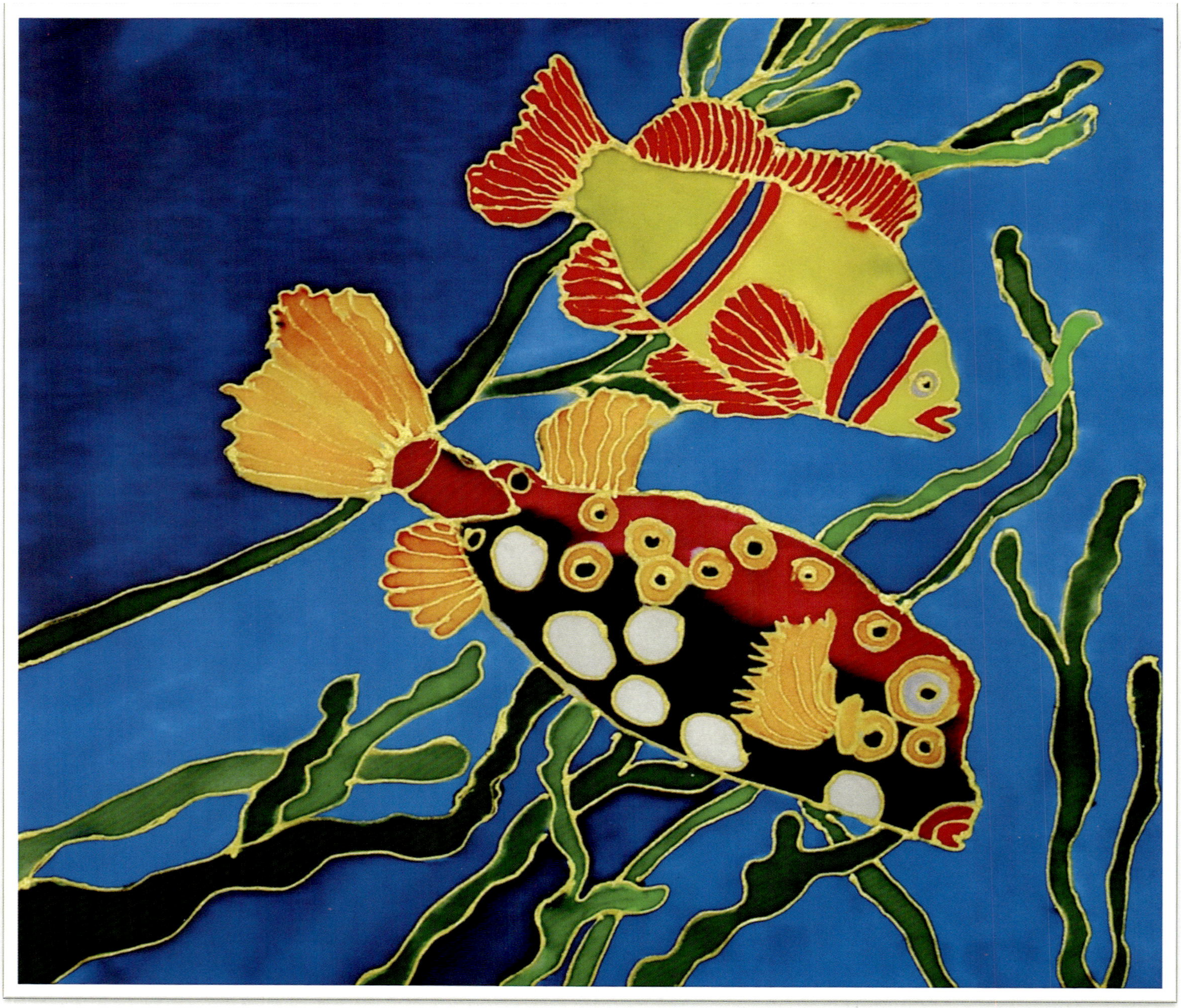

Different shades of grays

Find the formulas for different shades of grays and the black color.
Write down the formula for Angel Liana:

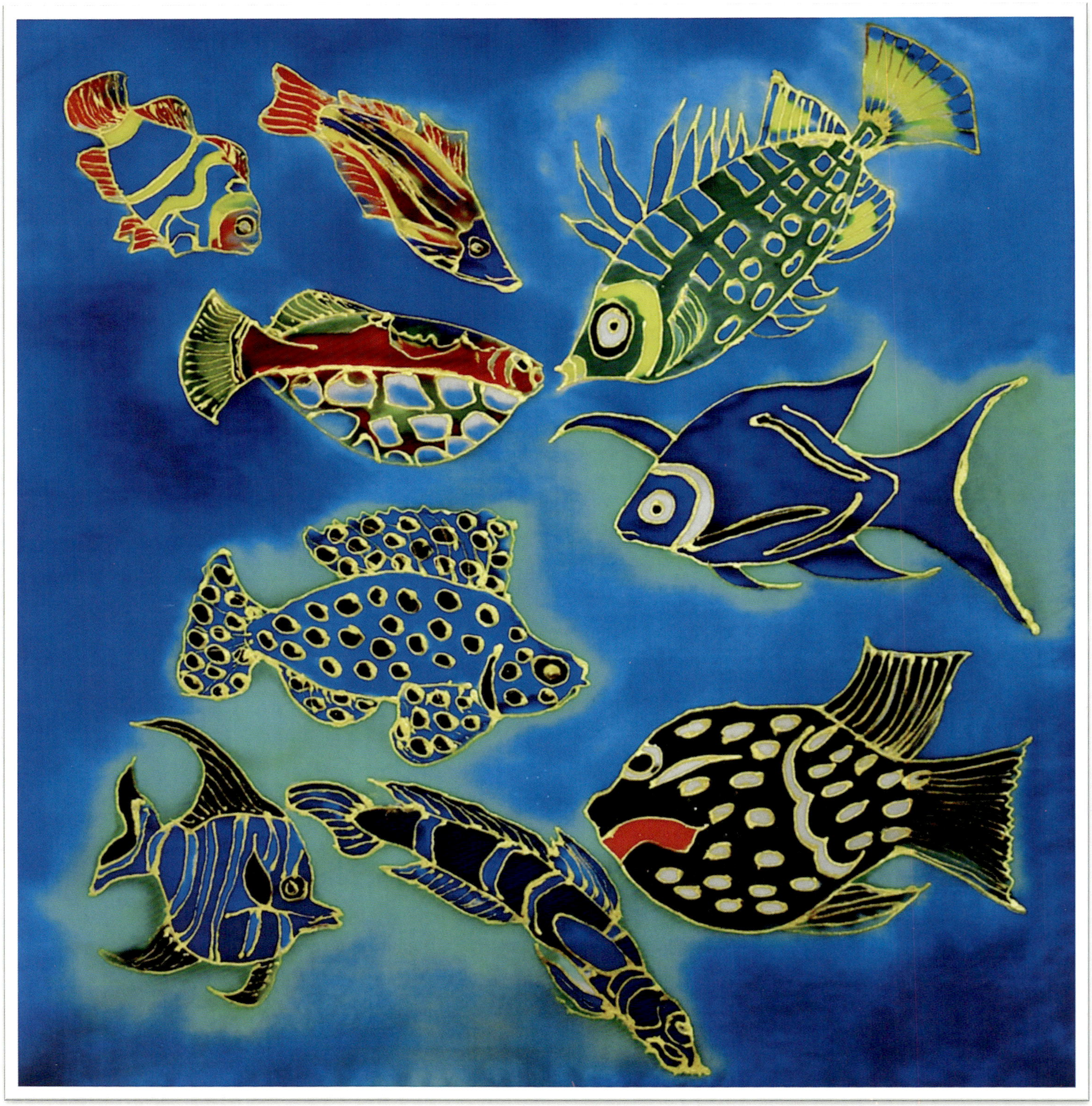

Book Five

Creating All the Other Shades of Colors

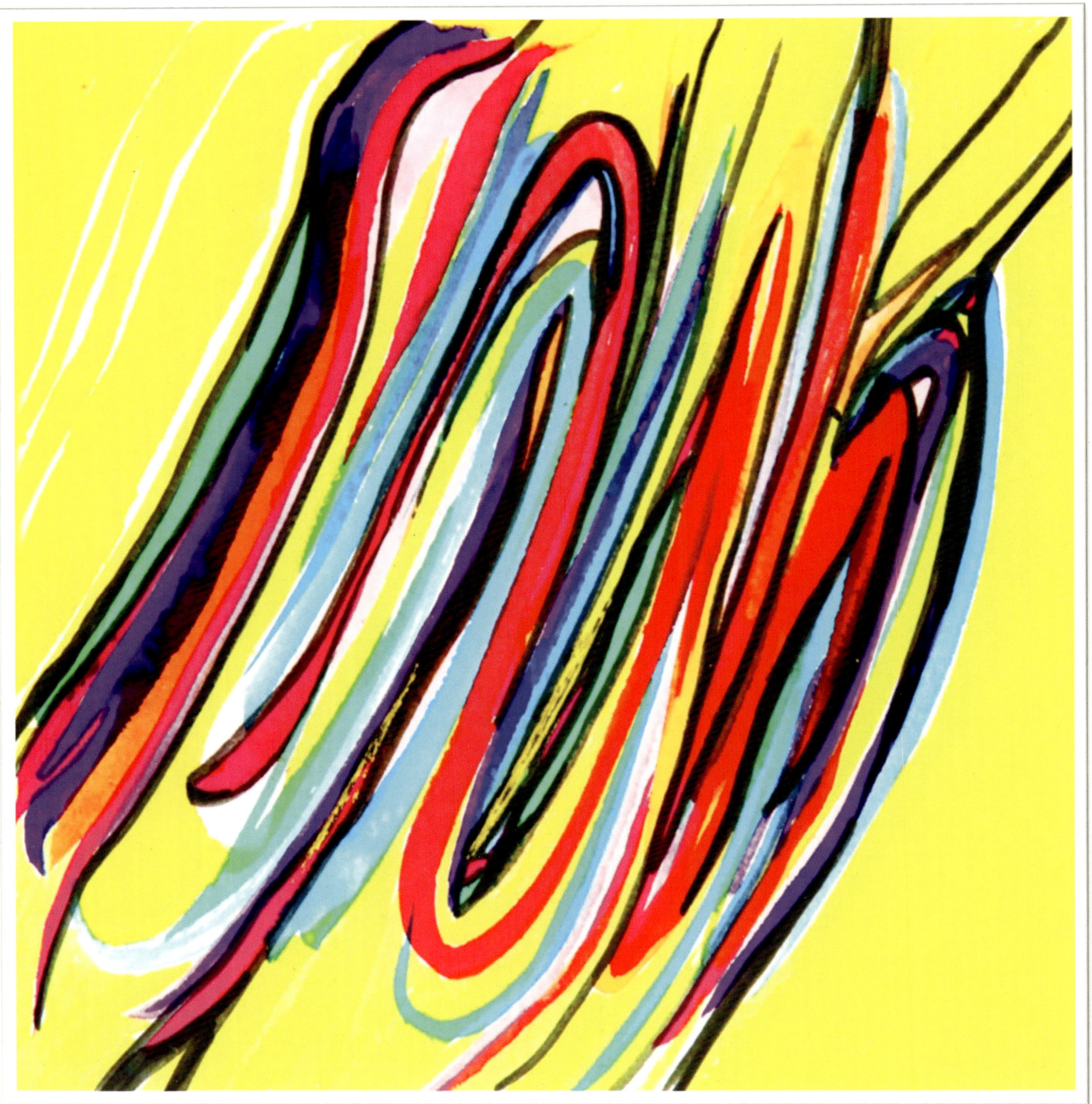

On the fourth week, most of the fish had become experts of color mixing. The large containers were filled with yellow, red, and blue primary colors. Some fish asked Angel Liana for additional mixing containers. And they started mixing different shades and dyed themselves in many colors.

Angel Liana reminded them by repeating the additional color mixing teachings:

In the color wheel, we can see the three primary colors:
Yellow, Red, and Blue.

In between there are the three secondary colors:
Orange, Green, and Violet.

The colors that are directly opposite each other in the color wheel are called complementary colors, which are the following:

Blue and Orange
Red and Green
Yellow and Violet

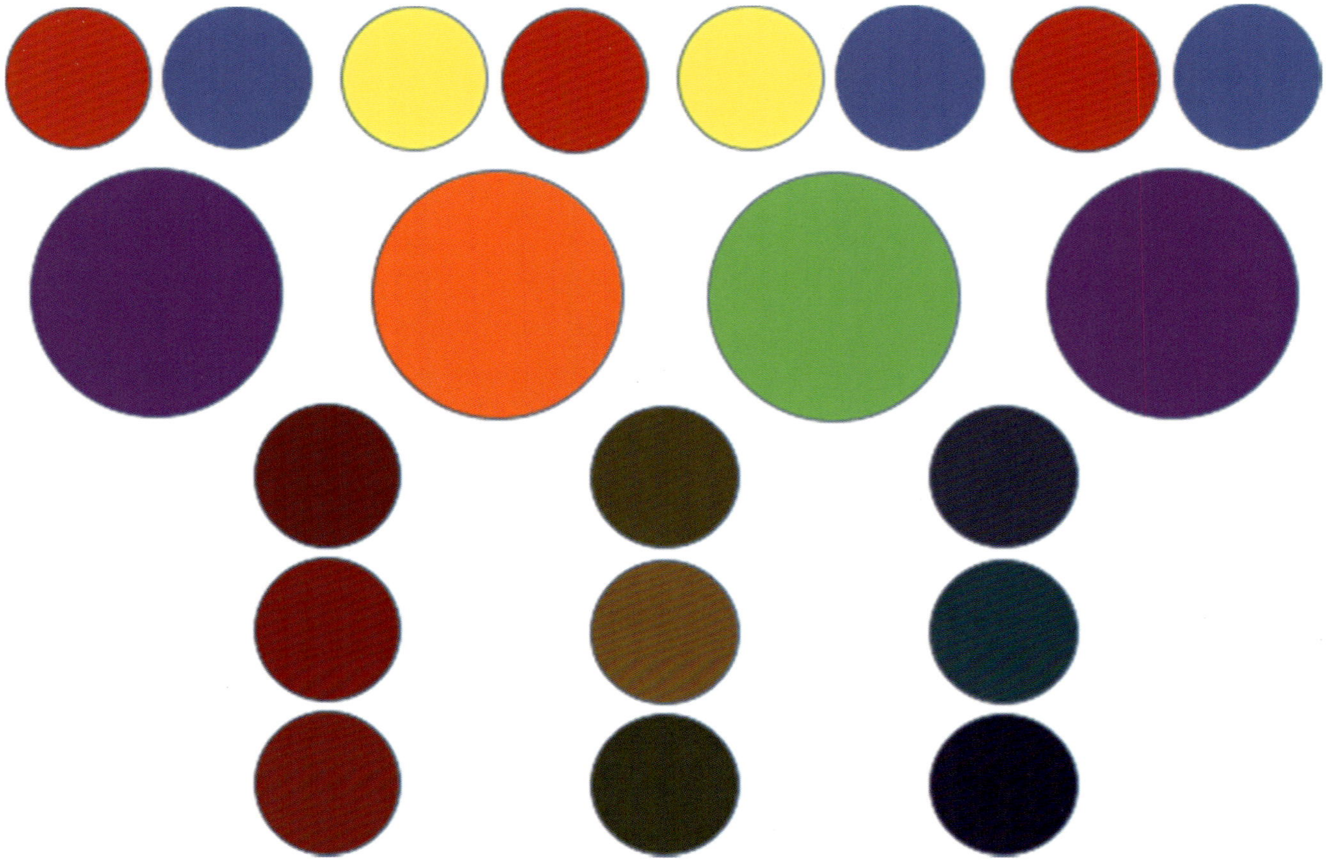

Primary colors: equal amount of 2 drops each

Red + blue	yellow + red	yellow + blue
Secondary colors:		
Violet	Orange	Green
Complementary colors		
2 violet + 2 red 6 violet + 3 red 3 violet + 6 red	2 red + 2 green 6 red + 3 green 3 red + 6 green	2 green + 2 violet 6 green + 3 violet 3 green + 6 violet

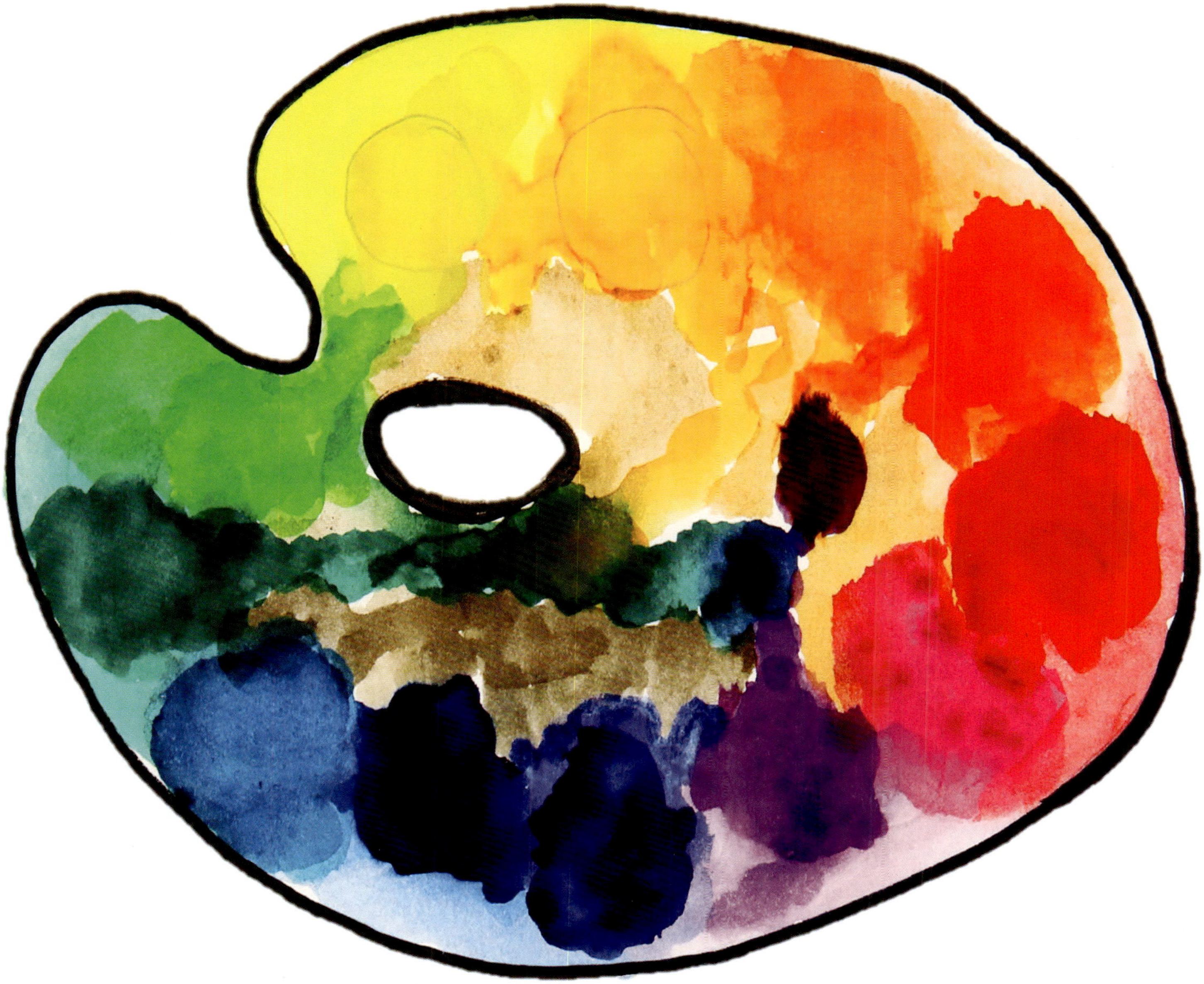

Now you can try to find more shades by mixing all these colors together.

Note: In order to obtain pastel (lighter) colors, just add water to the concentrated color. For example, if you add a lot of water to magenta, you will obtain a light rose color. Artistically, this is called a “tint”. By adding white to a color or adding water to lighten the color, we are making a tint. For example, baby blue is a blue tint.

When white paint is added to a color, we obtain the tint, but more of an opaque color. But if we add water to the paint to make it a lighter tint, the color is transparent and shiny.

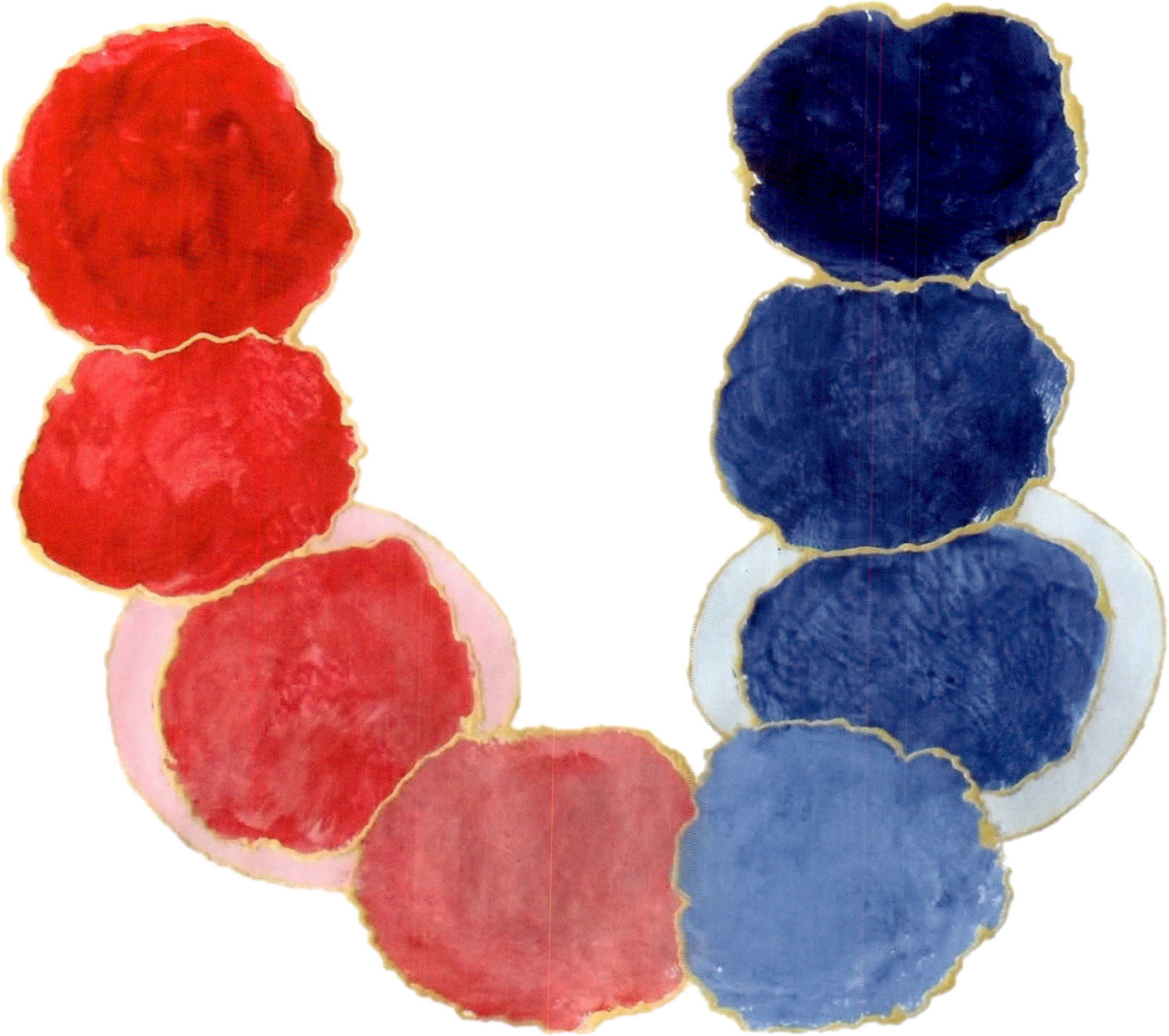

The two columns are blue and red first concentrate. The second color is the result of mixing to double quantity of water. The third column is obtained by adding much more water to obtain very pastel baby blue and pink.

The two on third column is red and blue each mixed to white paint that creates opaque pink and blue.

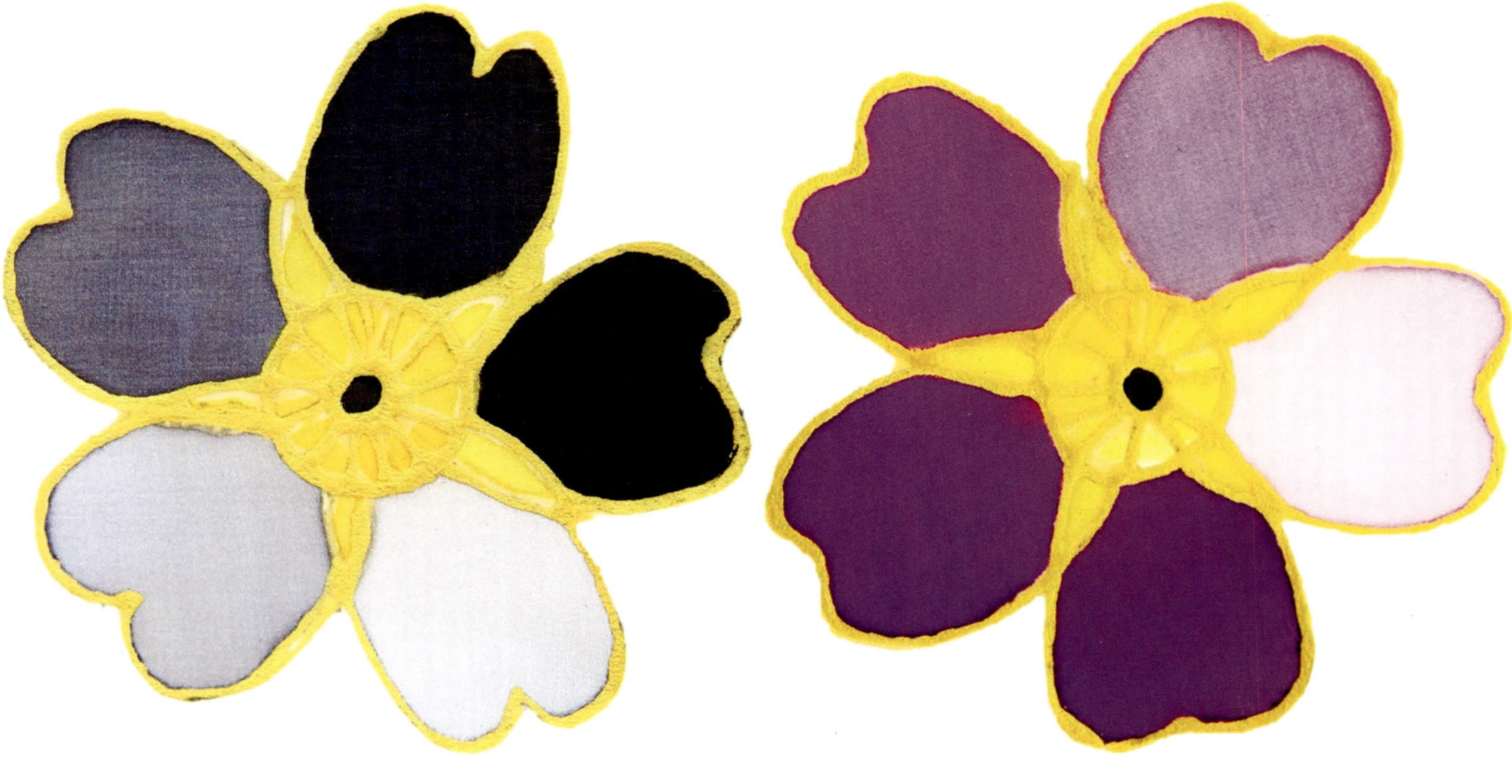

The petals of the two flowers above, gray and violet, in the middle are painted by first concentrate color and then mixed to a 25, 50, 75 and 100% of water.

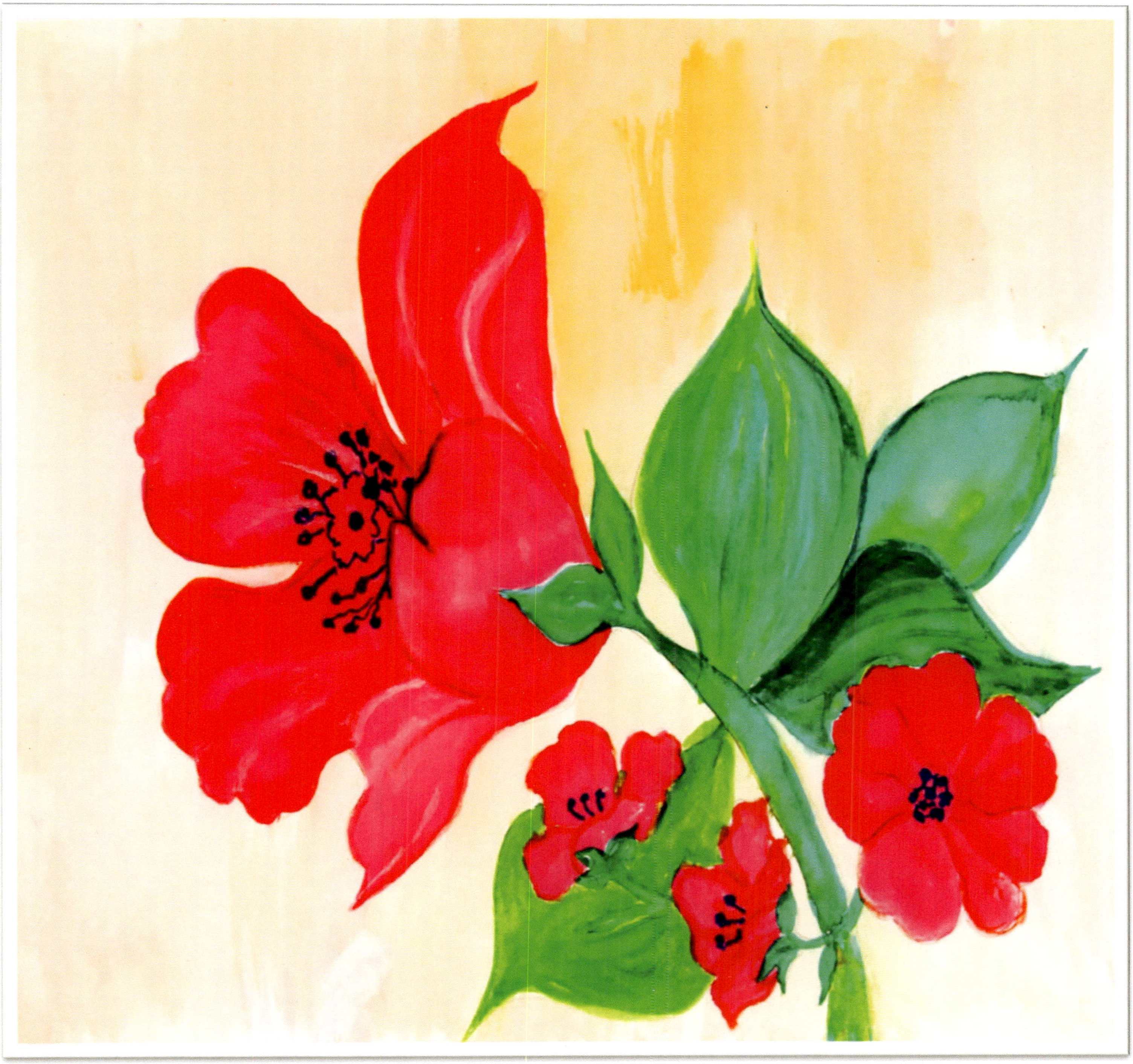

In this flower the same magenta color is used but with different tones of lighter and darker shades.

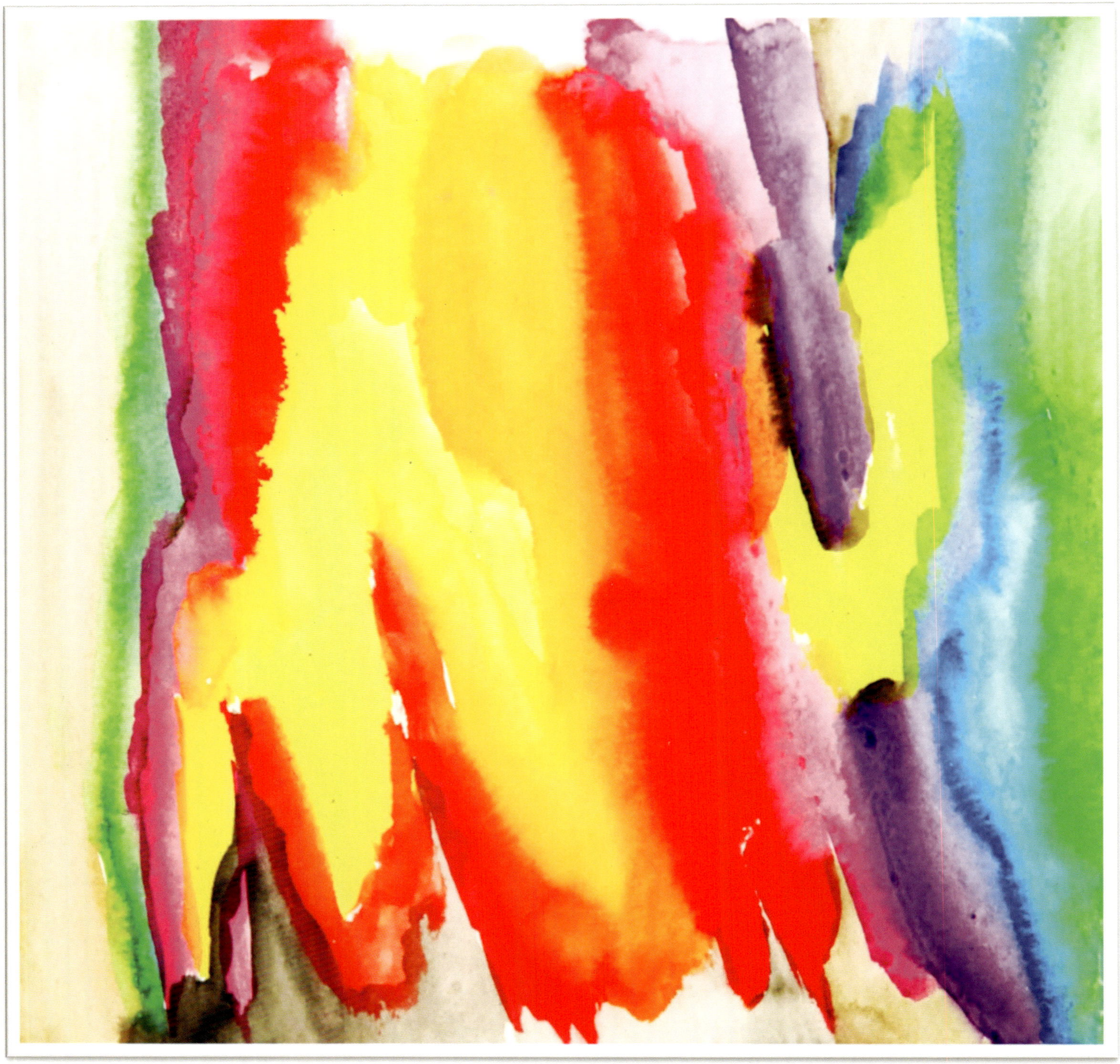

A composition of dark and light colors. Look what happens when the colors cross each other.

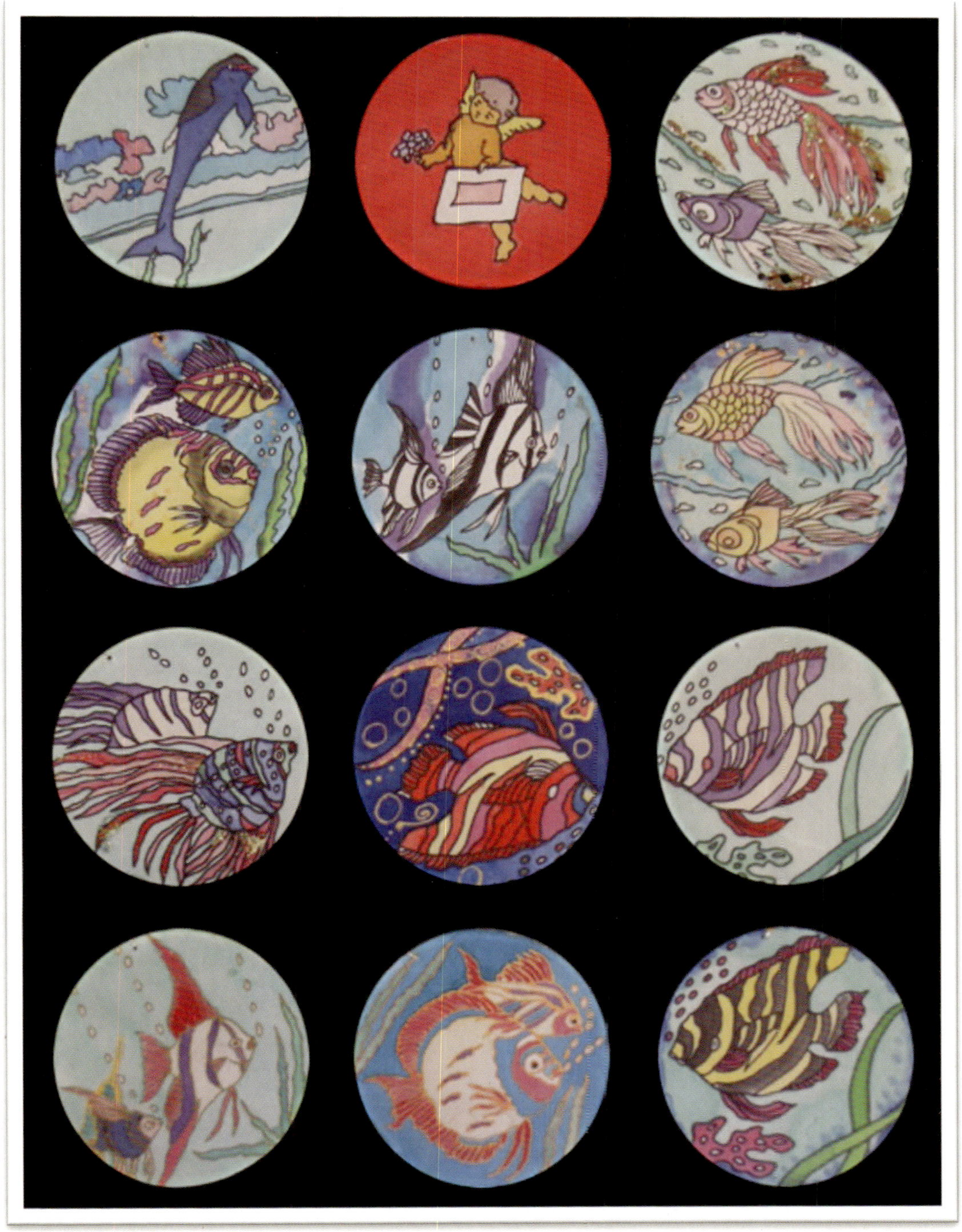

Play with colors and make decorative objects. As you can see, we have painted the same designs in different coloring, as the colors change they almost look like new designs.

One of the fun exercises is to make a color scale. The best way to work this project for the first time is to use black color.

First, put some drops of concentrated black color in the mixing cup. It will be easier to use a small flat brush. Mix the concentrated black color with the brush and draw a flat line on the top of the page. Add one drop of water to the concentrated black, mix with the brush, and draw a line under the first line, touching the end of the previous line.

Note: Do not leave white space between the black lines. It should show continuation of the shades. Do not wash your brush on each application. Since you are not changing colors, just mix the drop of water that has been added to the color and draw the next line.

Add more water each time to the black and draw the line. Continue doing this until you have painted your scale of the "gray shades" . The fun part is the end result. You can see that you have a scale, starting from very dark black to a very light gray, which almost reaches the white color.

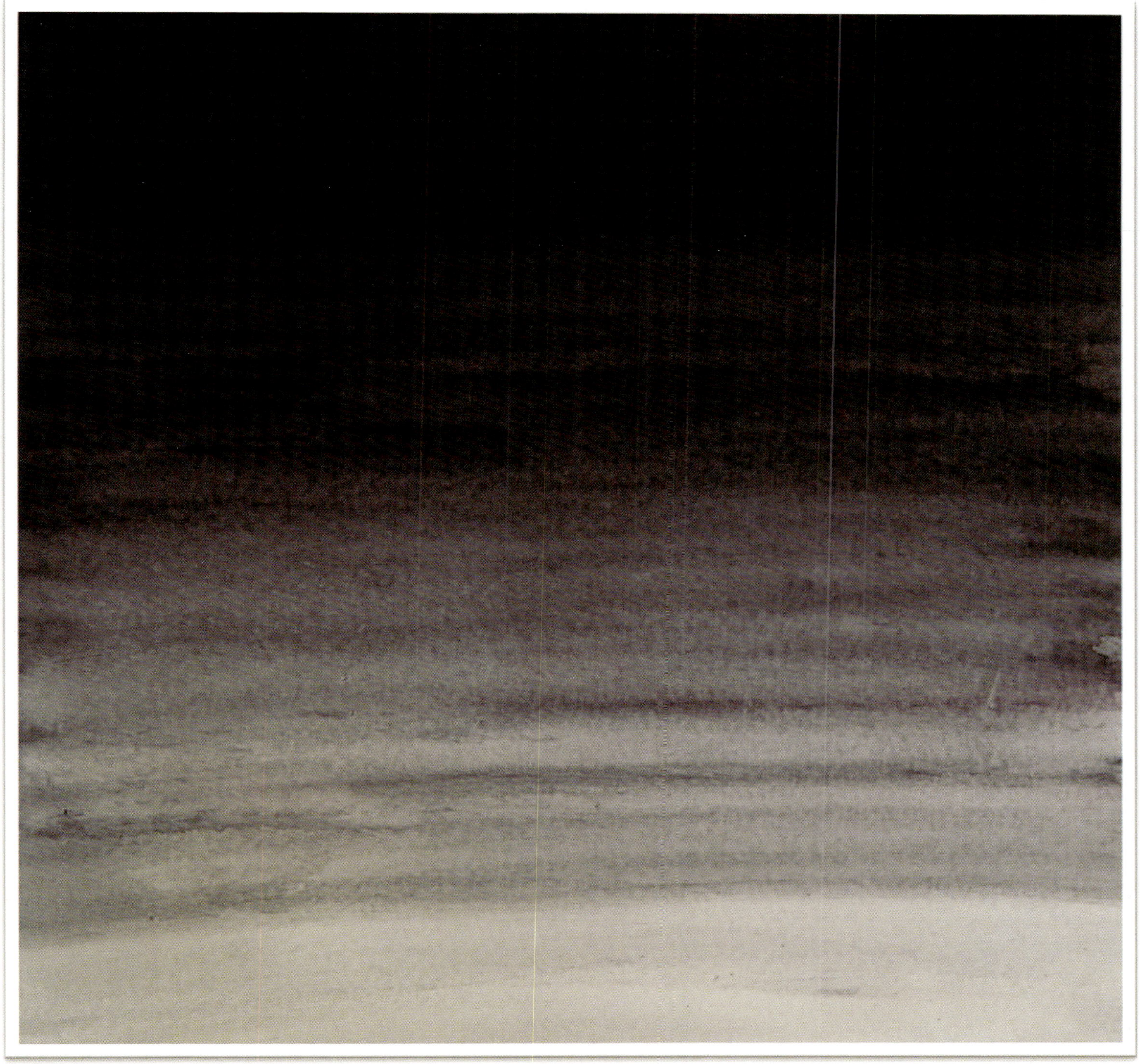

The gradation of grey scale

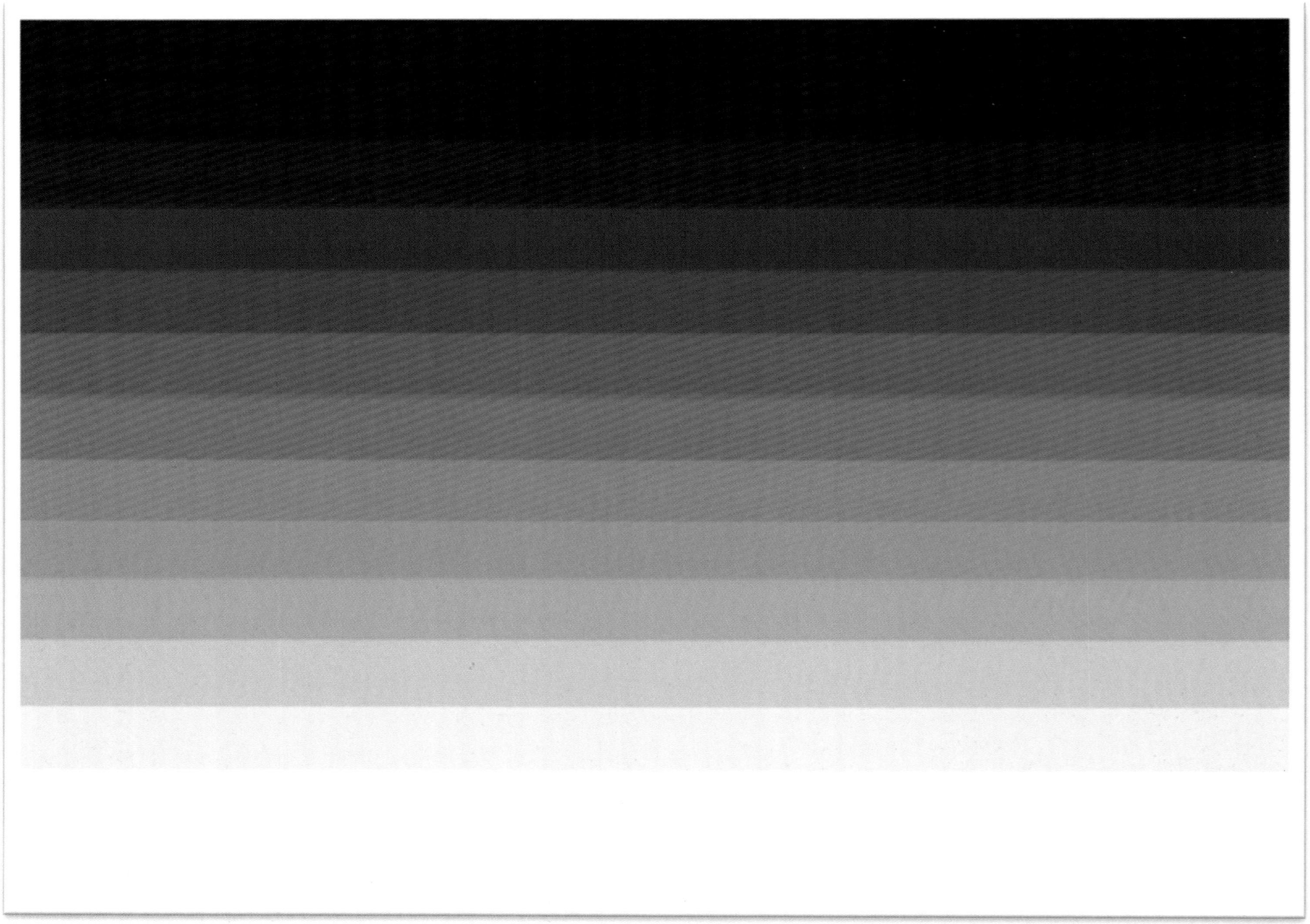

The gradation created on a computer

Now you can continue doing the scales for all other colors that you like. When the tone shows the relative darkness and lightness of a color, the scale is also called "gradation" in artistic vocabulary.

Angel Liana saw that many fish had learned the art of mixing colors and had changed their colors. She knew that her task was accomplished. She heard the call to return, and now the insects had heard of her talent and had requested to learn the art of mixing colors.

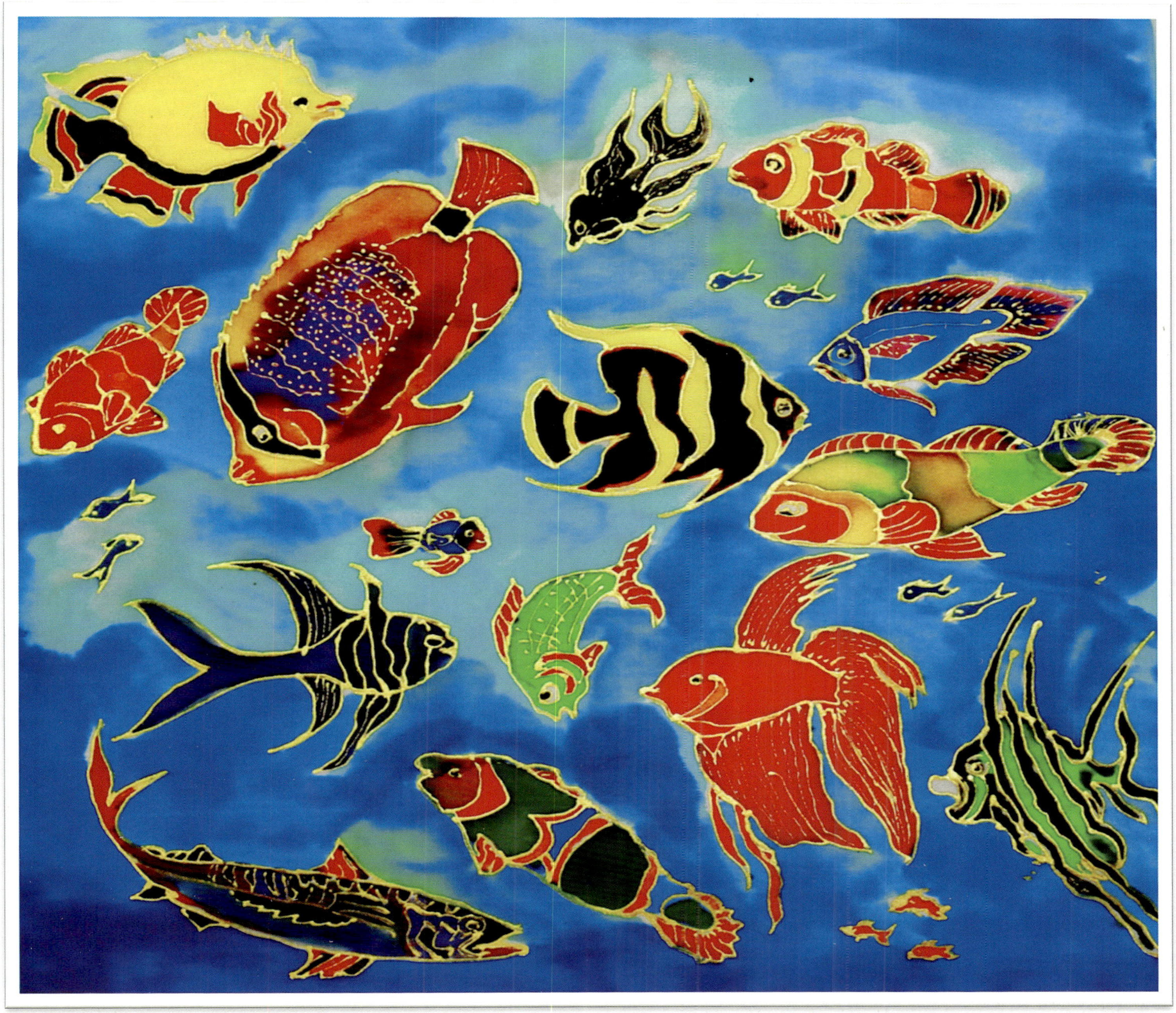

Angel Liana was sad to leave her new friends behind, but she was also happy to go back and meet her angel friends again. The colorful fish surrounded her to say goodbye. In order to show their appreciation, they put around her head a crown made of colorful sea plants, decorated with multicolor shells.

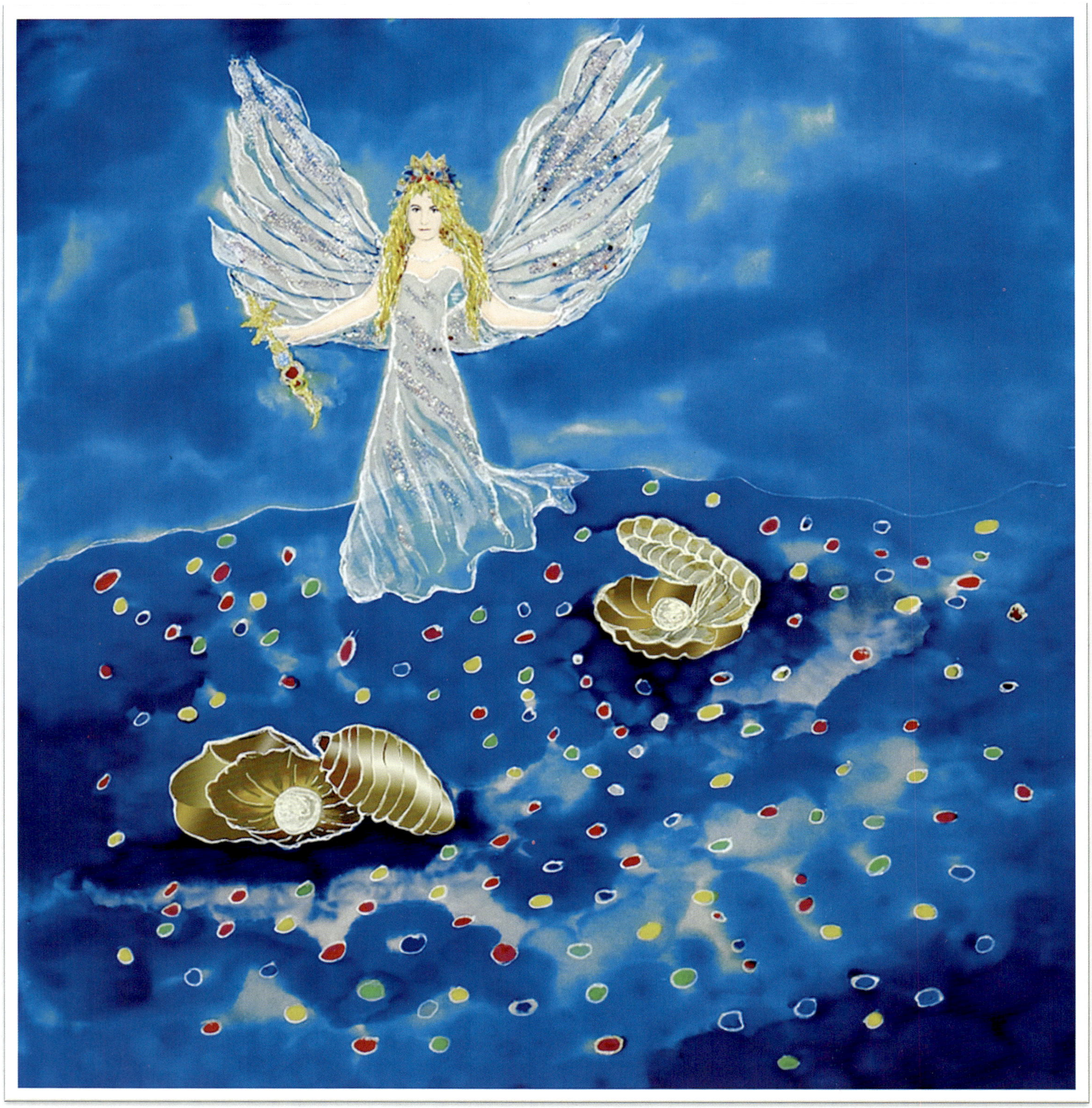

Angel Liana had shiny drops of tears in her eyes. When her tears dropped down into the water, the empty shells opened their mouths, immediately grabbed the tears, and closed themselves. This is how the beautiful pearls were created in her honor.

Since the queens, young girls, and women use beautiful pearl necklaces, precious bracelets and rings are made of all sizes of pearls. Many artists and crafters use shiny pearls in creating beautiful costumes and attractive objects.

Angel Liana said goodbye to all her new friends. As she pushed herself to the surface of the water, she gently hit the golden star on her fins and mermaid tail, and they immediately turned into her wings and legs. As she was flying toward the clear blue sky, all the fish hid themselves inside the water and sent air bubbles made by their mouths.

The surface of the water was covered with all sizes and colors of air bubbles, imitating party balloons in celebration of their friendship. Their bubbles were also a sign of appreciation for their teacher who had taught them the secrets and the art of mixing colors.

The End

A Word about Liana

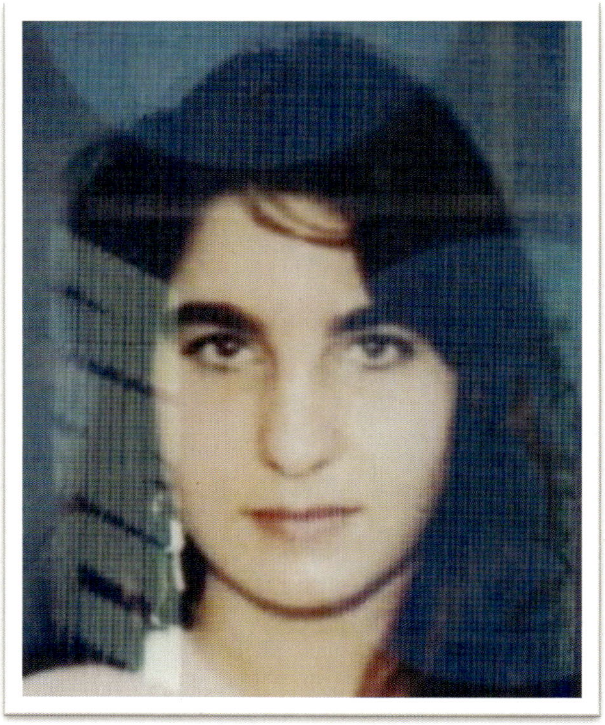

This is the last picture of Liana that arrived on the third day of her shiva, which was taken for her first driving license.

Since the fish coloring, Angel Liana has returned many times to the earth. She helped the insects with the art of coloring, then she taught the butterflies how to paint their delicate wings so beautifully. She has used her talents every time in order to embellish and make this world a better place to live in.

We were very fortunate to have Liana present among our family for 18 years. She lived on this earth as my daughter, your sister, your aunt, and a very helping and loving friend to many. She was a very beautiful girl, inside as well as outside. A good person's face always reflects the inner beauty, even if everything does not look as perfect as we wish.

She was a very sweet and talented girl. Liana was very hard-working; she was a studious girl at school, played the piano, and painted beautifully. She also had kept the sweet angelic voice that touched anyone who heard her singing. She loved sports and ran the Los Angeles Marathon many times, side by side with thousands of people. She loved and cared for all the students in her school and helped them with their homework and listened to their problems.

Sadly, a day prior to her departure to college, a drunk driver involved us in a car accident. The driver was exactly the opposite of Liana. He was bored with his life and did not know what to do in his spare time. Probably he was a lazy person who did not engage himself to study and acquire new knowledge, arts, and music, nor had he learned how to love others and help people around himself. Drinking alcohol was his only way of living.

Unfortunately, if we do not learn to fill our time with productive activities, we will end up hurting ourselves as well as others.

During the accident, Liana was probably called again for a new task, since she immediately left us and flew back to heaven, always ready for another mission.

Although we are saddened to lose Liana physically, she is always present in our hearts and mind. Apart from her kindness and beauty, she has left us many sweet memories, valuable gifts, and blessings.

Acknowledgements

Lia, I have written this book for you and *Ellie*,

and to all the girls and boys who like to study and learn new things in life.
I have written and painted this book with a lot of love and probably with the help of Liana for you and all the children. May you all live in a peaceful world showered with love.

Happy Birthday. I know that both of you know Liana in your hearts, because your mother and papa have told you stories about your aunt. It is so sweet when you mention her name and ask questions about Liana.

Angel Liana loves you very much; she watches and protects you from heaven. We all love you very much.

Angel Liana also joins us and wishes you a very Happy Birthday. She knows that you and all the children will grow to be beautiful, hard-working, and eager-to-learn people who will join God to embellish and make this world a much better place to live.

To the rest of the children who are reading this book:

I am sure you have also lost a very dear person in your young life. I know you are sad because of their absence, but as you can see in this book, although they are far, at the same time they are very close to you. You have experienced this on your birthdays, when you can feel a soft wind touching your skin. It is the way that they kiss you and wish you a Happy Birthday.

When you are sad and lonely, they are by your side and push you to paint, practice your music, read books, or go out and play with your siblings, friends, and neighbors. Many times you can find them in the books that you are reading.

And finally, let us change a word in our vocabulary: “lost”. When someone dies, the sentence that we hear is that we have “lost” him or her. In reality, we do not lose them; they go to a long trip. We have experienced so many good and bad moments and have so many memories of them. So don’t be sad. Be like Angel Liana: work hard, learn, practice, and help. In the Jewish tradition, when some one dies, they always say this meaningful and beautiful sentence:

“May his/her memory be for a blessing.”

And so it will be for you, too, as Angel Liana teaches you here. Use her color mixing secrets to paint a brighter world!

About the Author

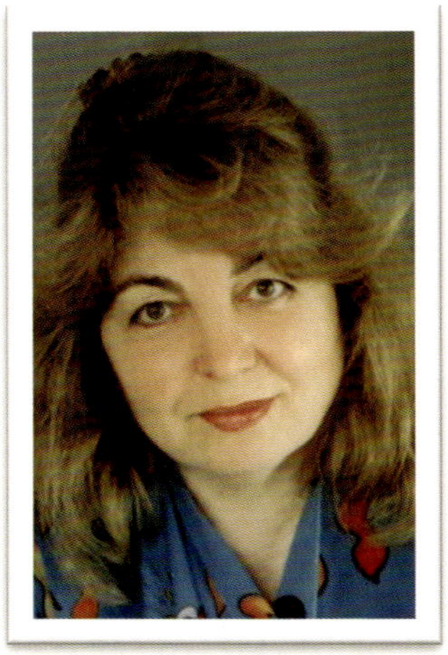

Dr. Rosemary Hartounian Cohen is a sociologist with a doctorate from the Sorbonne University, Paris. She is an award-winning author, a journalist, a motivational speaker, devoted wife, and mother. She is an accomplished artist who uses various mediums, including oil and charcoal, while her specialty is silk painting.

Dr. Cohen has taught university classes around the world and currently teaches at city colleges in Los Angeles. Her book design silk scarves and neckties was chosen by Publisher's Weekly as one of the best products presented at the Book Expo of America in 1999.

In 1985 Dr. Cohen founded Atelier de Paris in Los Angeles, and has served as its president ever since. She is fluent in several languages. She is the founder and director of the Liana Cohen Foundation, a charitable non-profit organization that organizes music competitions and festivals, encouraging youths to study music and arts, and provides the healing touch of music and arts to grieving families and survivors as well as victims of drunken driving, alcohol, and drug abuse.

Her many books include:

Korban – The Sacrifice of Liana
Terrorists or Martyrs
The Survivor, Translated and Published in:
Farsi (Iranian), Western Armenian, Easter Armenian, Turkish, and French.
The Mother of Jerusalem is Crying, (Winner of four book awards)
A Different Veil,
Anoush – The Daughter of King Shen

Supply Suggestions

In order to mix colors, I can suggest some simple tools:

Always before you start painting, cover the working area and the floor with plastic sheets

Wear an old dress or an apron

A roll of paper tower

Empty plastic jars

You will need to obtain:

Mixing cups tray / Color mixing palette

Simple soft brushes (You will need at least one brush for each color. If you use the yellow brush in red or blue color and wash it well, you can never obtain pure yellow color anymore because the end of the brush will keep some of old color. It is better to have also one color for each category of colors in order to be precise in the formula. Wash the brush with baby shampoo, rinse, and dry well).

Liquid paints (Thick paints can be used but they should be thinned with water. Read the label for: non-toxic)

Plastic droppers (to measure the colors)

A plastic container with water to wash brushes.

A notebook to write down the formulas. We have left some blank pages in the book for you in order to write down your formulas.

Note: All these supplies can be found at local art stores or ordered from:
www.AtelierDeParis.com

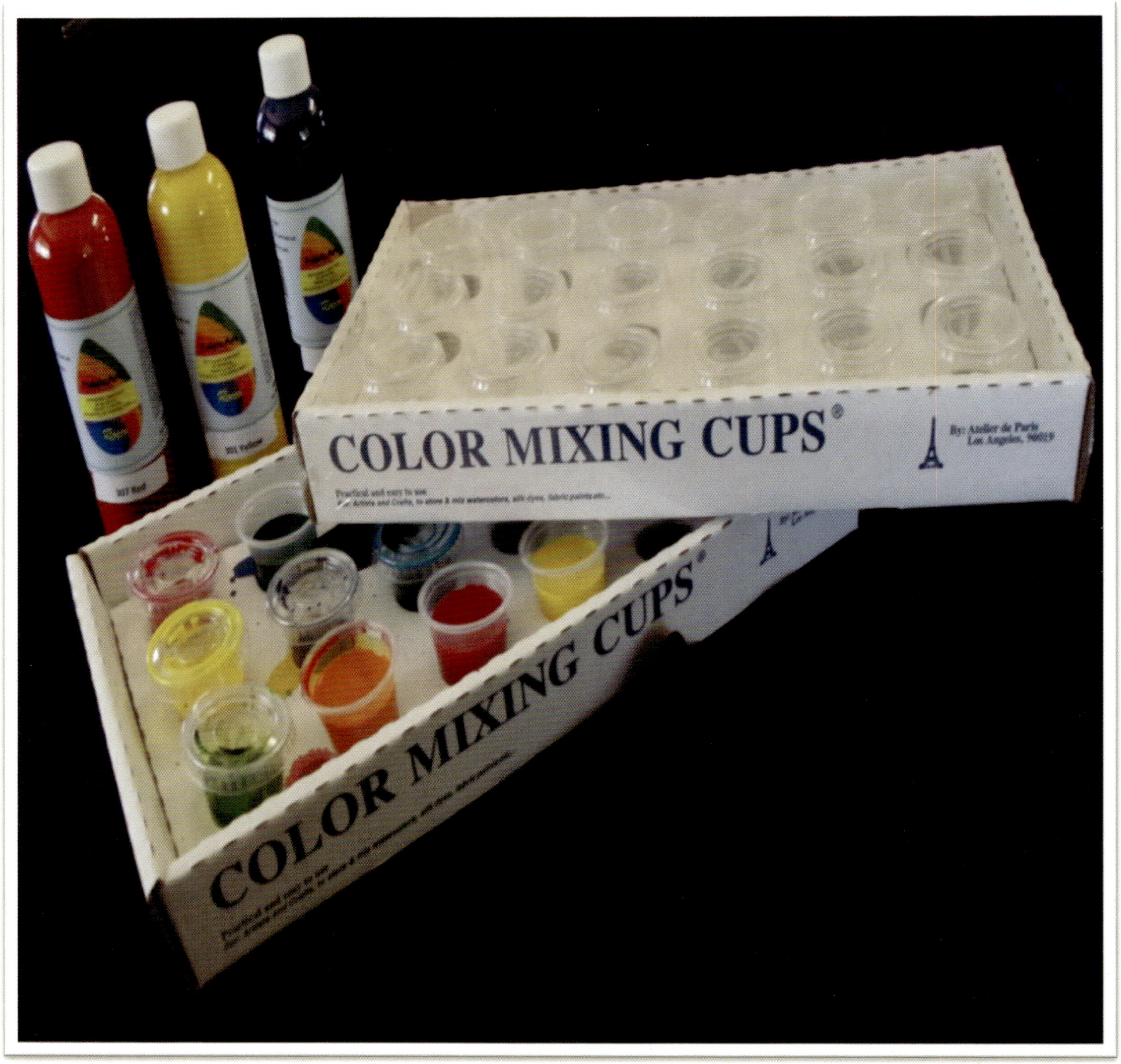

Mixing color cup tray

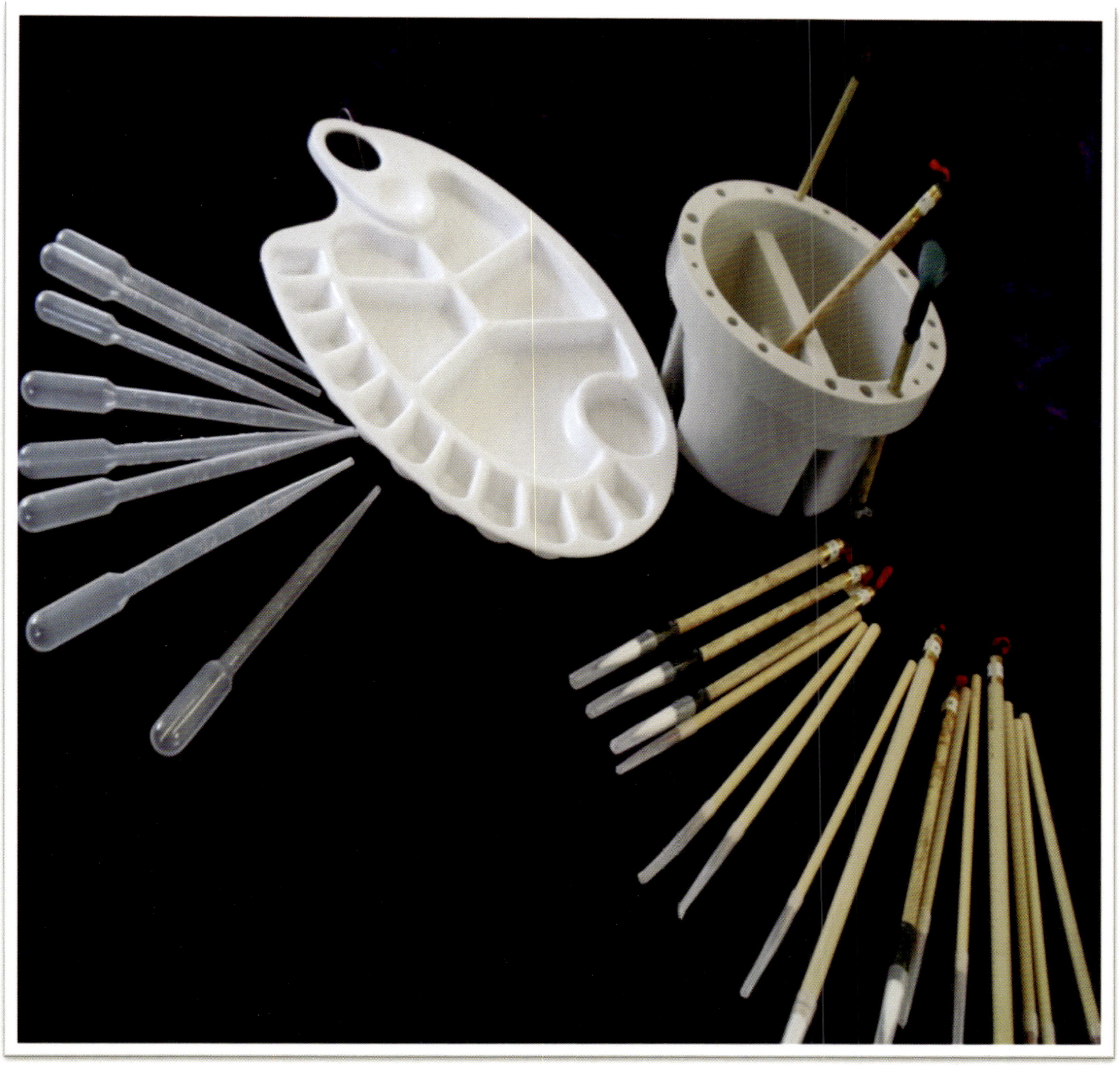

Painting palette, washing bowl, brushes and droppers

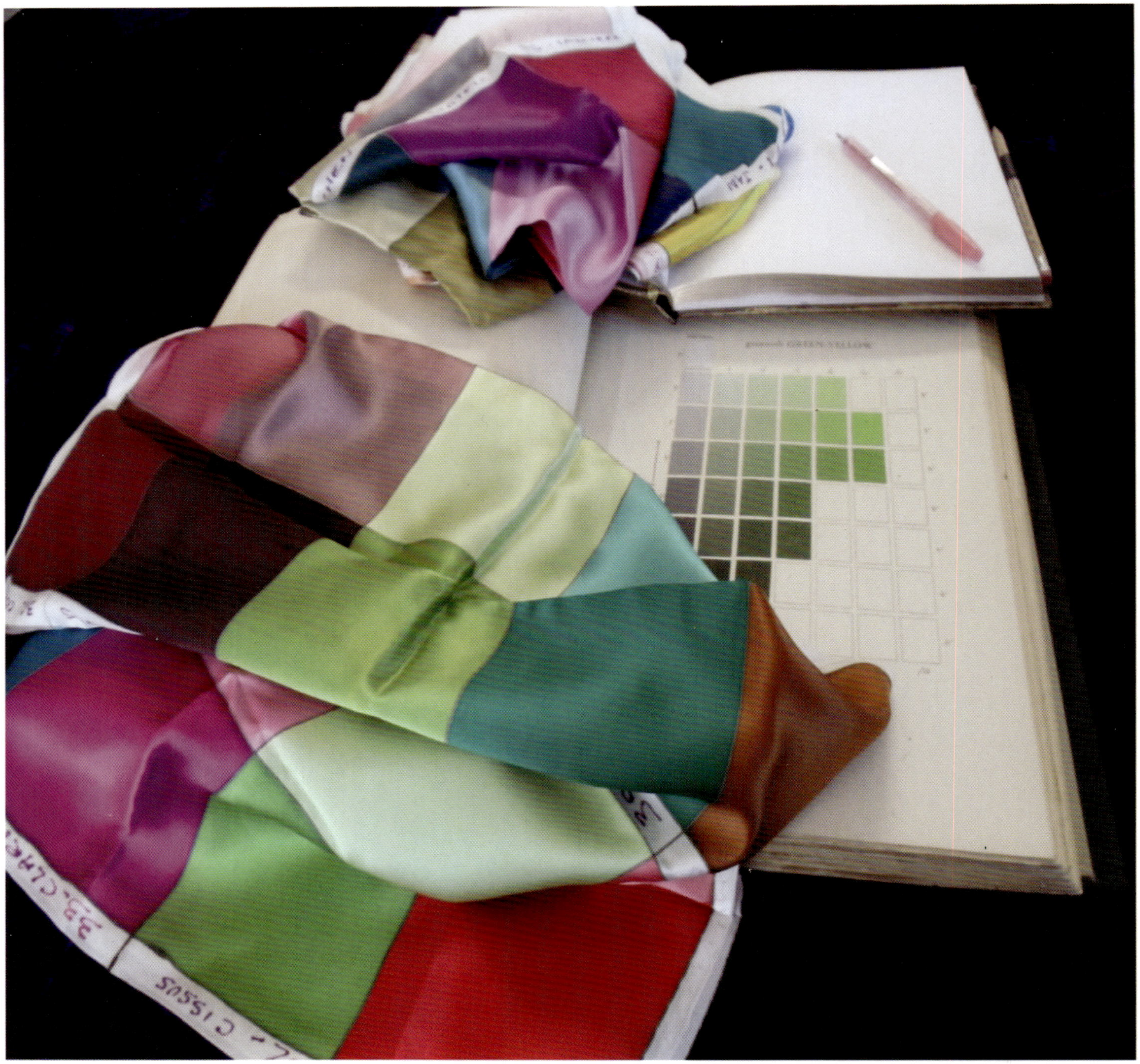

A blank notebook for writing down the formulas

Work Sheet

Write down your new formulas and a sample of each color:

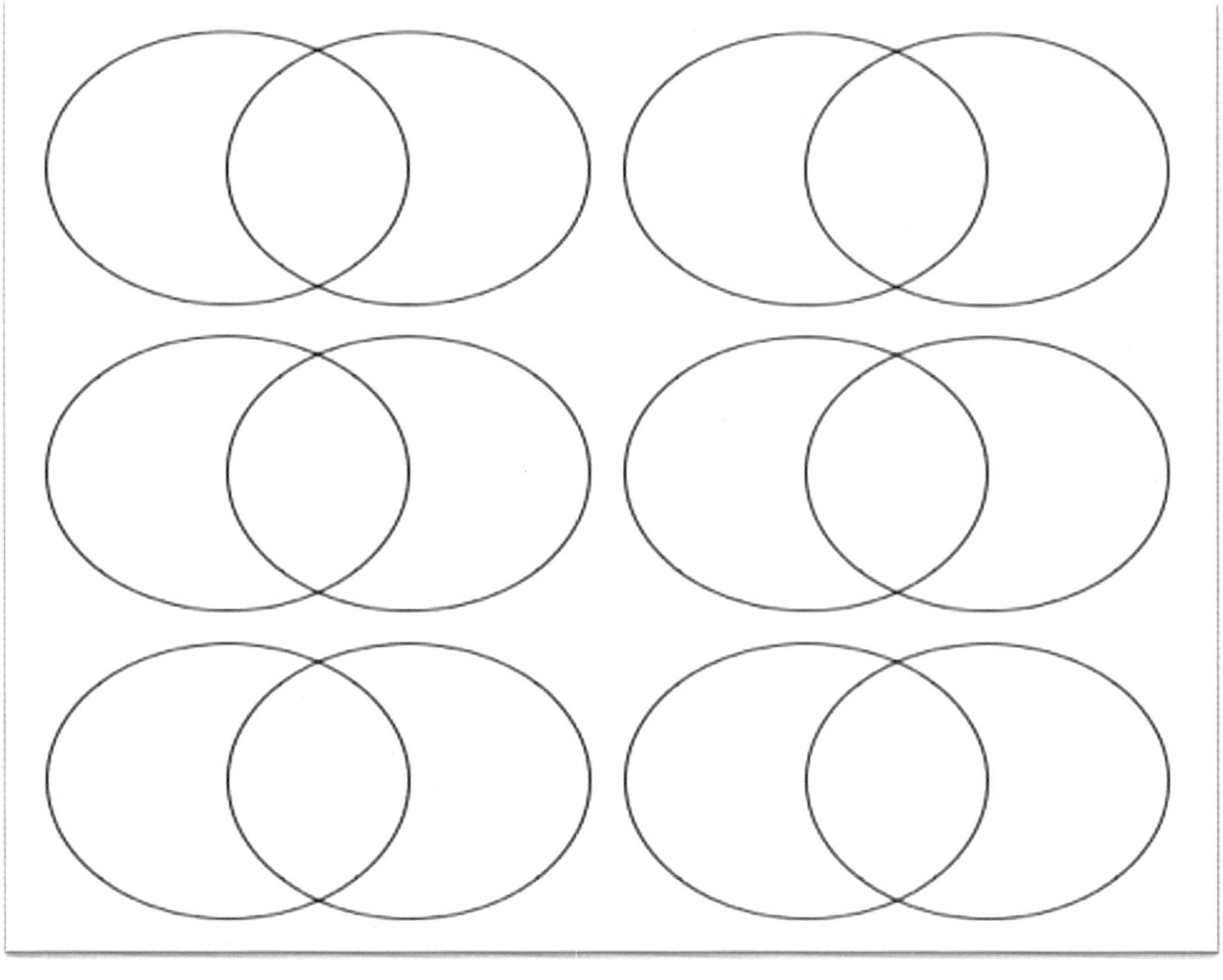

Choose two colors and paint each circle but in the middle mix them together and see the shades you will obtain.

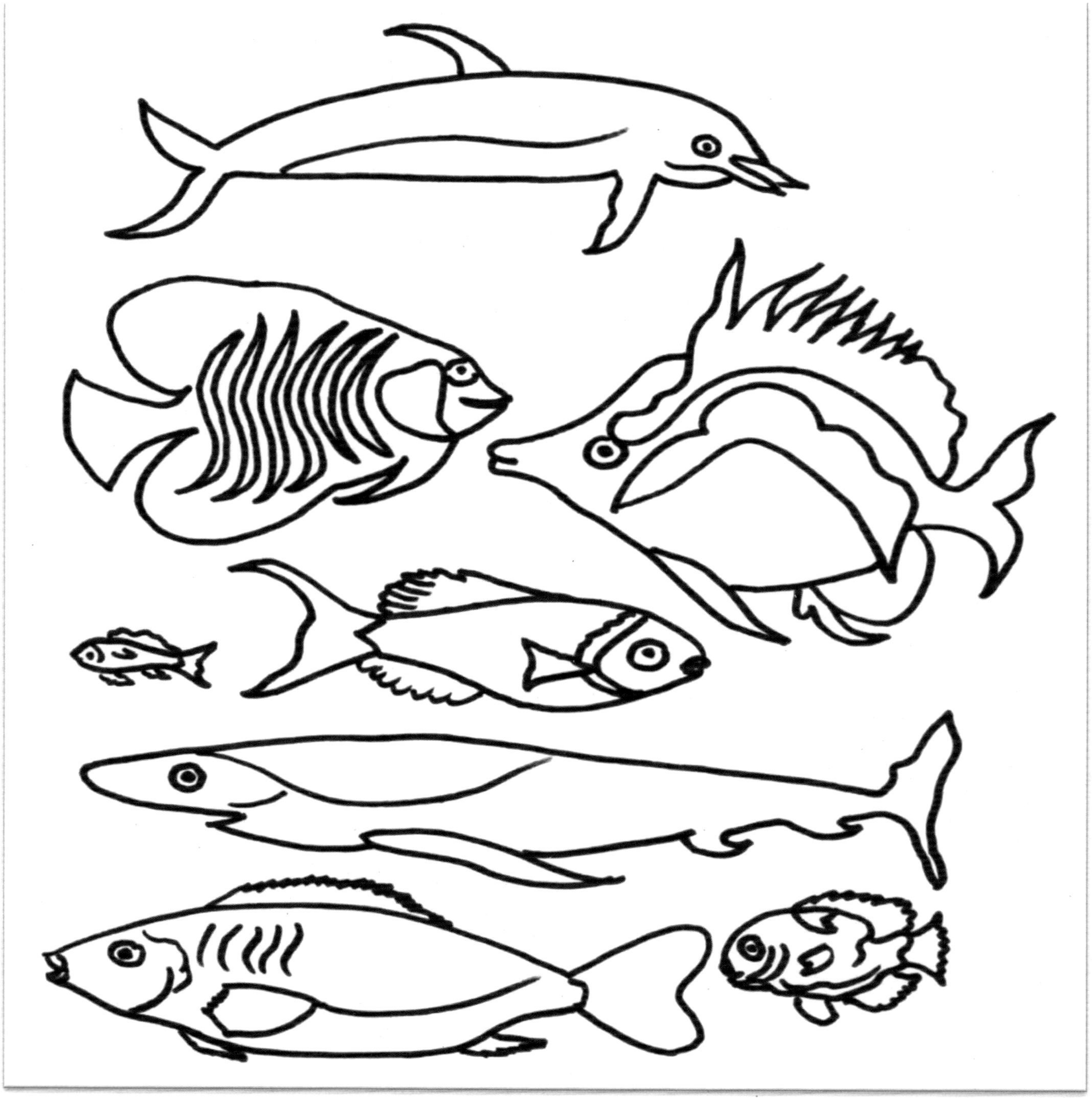

Color the fish with the new techniques that Angel Liana has taught you and write down the name of each fish.